The Challenge of
BLACK THEOLOGY
in South Africa

The Challenge of
BLACK THEOLOGY
in South Africa

edited by **BASIL MOORE**

John Knox Press
Atlanta, Georgia

First published in the United Kingdom, under the title *Black Theology,* by C. Hurst & Co. (Publishers) Ltd., 40a Royal Hill, Greenwich, London SE10 8SA

Published by John Knox Press, Atlanta, Georgia, 1974

© 1973, C. Hurst & Co. (Publishers) Ltd.

The Essays by Basil Moore and Sabelo Ntwasa have never previously been published. The other Essays in the work first appeared in *Essays in Black Theology,* published in 1972 by the Black Theology Project of the University Christian Movement, Johannesburg, South Africa

SBN 900966971

Library of Congress Cataloging in Publication Data

Moore, Basil, comp.
    The challenge of Black theology in South Africa.

    Contains essays, most of which first appeared in
Essays in Black theology, published in 1972.
    1. Theology--Addresses, essays, lectures.
2. Negroes in South Africa--Religion--Addresses,
essays, lectures. I. Title.
BR50.M63   230'.0968   73-16918
ISBN 0-8042-0794-1

Printed in the United States of America

CONTENTS

PREFACE

These essays were first published by the University Christian Movement in South Africa early in 1972. No sooner had they seen the light of day than they were banned. The South African Government saw in them a serious threat to the security of the State.

The original intention was to publish addresses given by South African thinkers at a series of conferences on Black Theology which were held during 1971 at the Wilgespruit Fellowship Centre near Johannesburg, the Edendale Ecumenical Centre near Pietermaritzburg, Natal, the Federal Theological Seminary at Alice, Cape Province, St Peter's Seminary, Hammanskraal, near Pretoria, and other centres in Zululand and the Transkei, as well as an address given at the South African Student Organisation (S.A.S.O.) conference in Durban. The articles by Professor Cone and Dr Omoyajowo were included when Sabelo Ntwasa was banned, and the editor wishes to express his gratitude to these authors. Their writings are included now as shedding light on the same problem as preoccupies our South African authors, but from different angles and in different styles.

Sabelo Ntwasa was the original editor of the first edition, but he was placed under house arrest while the material was at the printers, which meant that everything he had ever written was banned with him. His name had to be withdrawn as editor (to be replaced by that of Mokgethi Motlhabi) and his articles replaced. His articles are now therefore being published for the first time.

These actions of the South African Government give some idea of the situation against which the contributors to this collection of essays are working. They were not written as comfortable academic exercises, nor were they written to tickle the fancy of those uninvolved in the conflict in South Africa. They were written by black South Africans living in a situation of frightening oppression. And they were written for black South Africans exhorting them to participate in the struggle to throw off their chains.

One thing that may strike the non-South African reader is that they are totally lacking in a call to violent revolution. This is to be expected in a country where merely to discuss the possibility of violence is to fall foul of the law, and to advocate it carries severe penalties. But the reason for its absence lies deeper. These essays, each in its own way, call upon black people to throw off the shackles of their own internal enslavement as a necessary precursor to throwing off the external enslavement.

In South Africa the Christian Church has probably been one of the most powerful instruments in making possible the political oppression of the black people. While the white colonists were busy with the process of robbing the people of their land and their independence, the Churches were busy, however unconsciously, undermining the will of the people to resist. This was done in a number of subtle and not so subtle ways. In the first place the Church made it plain that everything African was heathen and superstitious barbarism. Conversion to Christianity meant rejecting traditional forms of dress, authority, social organisation, culture, marriage, medicine, etc. The black people were made to believe not that salvation is in Christ alone, but that salvation is in accepting the new white ways of living. The effect of this was to internalise in the black people a sense of the inferiority which inhered in them as Africans.

This was compounded by two other prominent strands in religious language. The first was the insensitive (or clever) interchangeability of 'black' and 'evil'. However natural this language might have been outside Africa, in Africa it was disastrous. The black person learned that the two terms were synonymous, but knew also that nothing could be done to change black pigmentation. It was therefore not difficult to persuade him that a black person is an evil (and inferior) person. This teaching was actively encouraged by the white Christians during (and after) the period of the Great Trek. The trekkers saw themselves as God's 'new Israel' leaving behind their enslavement in the Egypt of British rule in the Cape and crossing the wilderness into the new Promised Land inhabited by black Canaanites. This tradition has never died, and black people have been made to feel conscious that their blackness is a sign of their inferiority, as outcasts from the grace of God.

The second was the prominence given in Christian language to the 'nobility' of servitude. This is undoubtedly a prominent strand in Biblical language. But in the mouths of the new white masters it came to carry a different significance. It gave a religious and moral authentication to the social situation of masters and servants. Since there were only white masters and black servants, with the whites having no intention of becoming servants, this language served to reinforce and internalise the 'naturalness' and 'nobility' of black servitude. So the Church helped to colonise the minds of the black people, and in the Church as much as in the state all rule and leadership was assumed by whites with little resistance from the black people.

Black Theology is in revolt against the spiritual enslavement of black people, and thus against the loss of their sense of human dignity and worth. It is a theology in search of new symbols by which to affirm black humanity. *It is a theology of the oppressed, by the oppressed, for the liberation of the oppressed.* Unless this is understood from the outset, these essays will make little sense.

But the Black Theology movement must also be seen in a broader context. Under the present Nationalist Government in South Africa all forms of black political expression have been outlawed. Most leaders are languishing on Robben Island or in political prisons across the country. Those who have been lucky enough to escape are living in their thousands in exile. This has deprived the black people in South Africa of their most able leaders and spokesmen. Today almost the only platform open to black people is the Christian pulpit.

Unfortunately, under the weight of white leadership in the Church, black preachers have all received their training from white churchmen and theologians. Consequently the Gospel preached by these black preachers is firmly rooted in the perspective of whites. A major motivating force of the Black Theology movement is the self-education of these black clergymen. The question they persistently ask themselves is 'What is the meaning of the Gospel for those living not with

A*

their white bums in the butter, but with their black backs to the wall?' This question is easier to ask than to answer because for centuries theology has been the priviliged preserve of academics. What is significant now is that the question is being asked not by the rich old rulers but by the oppressed poor. Since Jesus was himself one of the oppressed poor, it is fascinating to read their re-assessment of him and of the Gospel of liberation.

But the significance does not lie in this fascination. It lies in the impact that this re-interpretation is going to have on the millions of black Christians in South Africa who, Sunday by Sunday, flock to the churches to listen to black preachers. If they are able to kindle a myriad of sparks of angry resistance to their dehumanisation, who will be able to stop the blaze, even without the outstanding leaders of yesterday?

The South African Government has seen this threat and has begun to act with severe retribution against some of the people involved. The white church too is afraid, and the Black Theology movement can expect little sympathy or support from that quarter. But there is now no stopping the tide. You can arrest and imprison leaders and ban books, but you cannot stop ideas. Some of the ideas at work today are contained in this collection of essays. Perhaps most of their authors will be silenced. But we are privileged to share in a new theology in the making.

BASIL MOORE

London, November 1972

ADDENDUM

As this book was going to press, news was received that Steve Biko and Nyameko Pityana were banned in March 1973 under the Suppression of Communism Act.

Grateful acknowledgment is made for permission to reprint James Matthews' poem, which appeared in the volume *Cry Rage*, published by U.C.M., Johannesburg, in 1972. The book was banned by the South African censors in March 1973. We have entitled the poem 'Christians'; previously it had no title.

NOTES ON CONTRIBUTORS

Basil Moore, a Methodist clergyman, is a graduate of Rhodes University, Grahamstown, and a past general secretary of the University Christian Movement in South Africa; he was banned under the Suppression of Communism Act, and is at present co-ordinating secretary of the British Student Christian Movement in London. *Dr Adam Small*, a Coloured poet, is head of the Department of Philosophy, University of•the Western Cape, Bellville, South Africa. *Sabelo Ntwasa* was an Anglican ordinand at the Federal Theological Seminary, Alice, Cape Province, and director of the Black Theology Project of the University Christian Movement until he was banned to his home town of Kimberley before completing his studies. He is thus under house arrest for five years. *Dr Manas Buthelezi*, formerly lecturer at the Lutheran Seminary at Umpumulo, Natal, is pastor of a Lutheran congregation at Pietermaritzburg. *Steve Biko* was the first president of the South African Students Organisation (S.A.S.O.) and is a medical student in what is officially known as the 'Wentworth Medical School' but known by its students as the 'Black Section', at the University of Natal. *Dr James H. Cone*, a black American, is assistant professor of theology at the Union Theological Seminary, New York. *Nyameko Pityana*, an arts graduate of Fort Hare University, Alice, became secretary-general of S.A.S.O. after his expulsion from that university. *James Matthews* is a Coloured South African, living in Cape Town. He is in his forties and has had verse and short stories published previously; he at present works as a journalist on *Muslim News*. *Bonganjalo Goba*, a graduate of the Federal Theological Seminary, Alice, is a Congregational minister in Cape Town. *Mokgethi Motlhabi*, a former student for the Catholic priesthood, refused to return to St Peter's Seminary at Hammanskraal, Transvaal, when all students were suspended following a strike. He became acting director of the U.C.M Black Theology Project after the banning of Ntwasa: the U.C.M. no longer exists, but he is now director of the Black Theology movement in the Johannesburg-based Association of Black Churchmen. *Dr Akin J. Omoyojowo*, a Nigerian, is a lecturer in theology at the University of Ibadan. *Dr Mongameli Mabona* is a Catholic priest and lecturer at St Peter's Seminary, Hammanskraal, Transvaal. *Ananias Mpunzi*, a graduate of the Federal Theological Seminary, Alice, is an Anglican priest in the diocese of Kimberley.

I

WHAT IS BLACK THEOLOGY?

by Basil Moore

Introduction

The term 'Black Theology' was coined in the United States where it is to a large extent a theological response by black theologians to the emergence of Black Power. This is best exemplified in James Cone's earlier work *Black Theology and Black Power*. More recently it has become an aspect of the development of a theology of liberation. Here it has been the contribution of black theologians to the theology of liberation from the perspective of the Black American. This trend is best exemplified in the later work of James Cone, *A Black Theology of Liberation*.

While the catch title 'Black Theology' has been imported from the United States into South Africa, the content of American Black Theology has not been imported with the title. This is to be expected, for while there are many striking parallels between the situation of the black man in America and South Africa, the differences are almost as striking as the parallels.

Thus what we need to look at here is not what 'Black Theology' is in its American context, but what it is in South Africa. This is extemely difficult. There is no standard, authoritative text book on the subject in South Africa and there are no established 'authorities'. The author certainly does not pretend to be such an 'authority' and does not wish to be regarded as such. As a consequence no summary of what black theologians are saying can be presented. The best we can do is try to come to grips with what we think Black Theology ought to be about, and look a little more closely at the situational factors which have made it necessary.

The Death of Multi-Racialism

Perhaps the most significant factor which has made the emergence of Black Theology possible in South Africa is the growing mood among blacks against multi-racialism. It is necessary to look closely at some of the chief reasons for this new mood to counteract the easy and superficial charge that it is simply black racialism, and to counteract the other equally superficial charge that 'Black Theology' is a symptom of the successful brain-washing of the 'Separate Development' politicians.

When the National Party came into power in 1948, the Churches – especially the so-called 'English-speaking', 'multi-racial' Churches – began to show signs of alarm. Opposition to this officially sponsored racism began to be voiced by some of our ecclesiastical leaders. This was strange, because one got the impression that legalised racial discrimination had come into being with the 1948 elections. But this was not true. Racial discrimination was on our statute books long before 1948. Why then did this new note of opposition come from the established churches?

Perhaps one of the reasons for this was that the pre-Nationalist racism had been implemented by the 'English' political parties. In the long history of English-Afrikaner conflict in South Africa it is natural that the English Church leaders would have felt some sort of solidarity with the 'English' parties even if they were not actually members of them. When the Afrikaner opposition party came into power, it is again natural that the English Churches and churchmen would have felt identified with the new opposition group. This made it much easier for them to express opposition to the ever-increasing array of racist legislation. It is always easier to blame 'them' rather than 'us' for racism. As a consequence the character of the Church's opposition was fundamentally more anti-National Party than anti-racist. It remains true that the Church has never seriously come to grips with its own racism.

Whatever the reasons for the rising tide of Church-based opposition, it led to an increasing demand within the churches for multi-racialism. This, of course, was very limited. Little or no attempt was made within the Churches to alter the white-dominated power structures of the Churches. All authority still resided in white hands. Whites continued to be appointed as bishops, general secretaries, etc., and continued to control financial concerns, publications and theological education (especially that of blacks). But alongside this white control arose the clamour for multi-racial contact. So there emerged a plethora of multi-racial meetings – synods, conferences, discussion or study groups, student movements, etc.

The religious rationale for this 'contact', which also had its secular counterpart, was 'reconciliation'. Against the rising tide of racialism the Churches or their leaders came to see the crucial need as being for 'reconciliation' between blacks and whites. This need for 'reconciliation' led to an almost pathological 'got-to-get-me-a-black-man-to-find-out-what-he-is-thinking' attitude among many whites.

The effects of this multi-racialism were not all negative. It is true that this 'reconciliation contact' did enable a few whites (very few) to move from their racialist inheritance to an open desire for non-racialism. But it is equally true that many more became rather sickening paternalists and charitable 'do-gooders'. Whether there was any positive effects on blacks in this multi-racialism is debatable. What is not debatable is that for blacks generally it was disastrous because it took place in the context of South African society, a society in which there is a vast gap in wealth and education between blacks and whites. In the main the whites who were ready, willing and able to enter into the 'dialogue' with blacks were highly educated and, even by white standards, wealthy. It was natural that the 'dialogue' they sought was with blacks who could more or less easily enter into their sophisticated discussions (i.e. the tiny upper-upper educated black élite), and whose standards of living compared favourably with their own (i.e. the tiny upper-upper economic black class).

As a consequence the 'reconciliation' that took place was phony. What happened in effect was that 'class' loyalty took over from race loyalty. Black and white distinctions paled before the common bond of wealth and education. This class character was by no means peculiar to the religious forms of multi-racialism. Class cohesion marked the now-defunct Liberal Party, and marks the Progressive Party even more strongly.

Having this class character the effect of multi-racialism was

to draw the upper crust of black society off from the masses
and then to graft it on to the white middle-to-upper class. But
the illiterate, poor and starving black masses were left as
leaderless and excluded as ever. The black élite who enjoyed
the delights of black-white 'dialogue' turned away from the
black masses and seldom ploughed back into their people
their resources of intellect and skill. Show us the black churchmen who have taken time off from attending multi-racial
meetings to take seriously the de-humanising plight of the 75
per cent illiterate blacks, and to gain the skills to devote themselves to enable this mass of their people to read and write.
Where are the black churchmen who are gaining the skills to
serve their people in their waterless starvation on South Africa's
rural wastes to enable them to feed themselves and their children? Which black churchmen are to be found at Bantu
Commissioners' offices with a real knowledge of the host of
influx control laws, helping their people to find a home and
hold their families together?

The answer to all these questions is that such leaders are as
rare as love in the South African parliament. Courting rich
whites they have lost contact with the poor blacks. 'Reconciliation' between the races has been gained, if at all, at the expense
of 'reconciliation' between the potential black leaders and the
forgotten black masses. This, above all else, has been the black
tragedy of our middle class multi-racialism.

If our bourgeois multi-racialism has been disastrous for blacks
in our South African situation, it has also been disastrous for
the whites involved. Little needs to be said about this here but
it is sufficient to note that while whites have tried through these
'contact' meetings to become involved in helping others (i.e.
blacks) – usually with lashings of paternalism – they have
seldom, if ever, got together to ask themselves what is happening to themselves. Trained to be oppressors from their tenderest
years in order to fit into their roles in our capitalistic and
authoritarian society, they have seldom stopped to ask themselves what they have lost in human warmth, tenderness,
sympathy, sorrow and caring. Even less have they asked themselves why it has been necessary to destroy this human tenderness. Thus they have not seen that it is impossible to be an
emotionally whole human being and a cold, calculating, money-

and power-grabbing businessman, politician, bureaucrat or ecclesiastical authority at the same time.

The question our liberal white multi-racialists have asked is what are 'they' (the government) doing to 'them' (the blacks) and not the vital, fundamental question 'Who am I?' and 'What is happening to me as a human being in this situation?'

Like most of us, I am prepared to trust and stand alongside a man who is fighting for himself and his own freedom if I know that his freedom is bound up with mine. I cannot whole-heartedly trust a man who is fighting for me, for I fear that sooner or later he will tire of the struggle. In other words, if both black and white are able to focus for themselves the character of the freedom struggle in South Africa, they stand a better chance of being allies than they do in the false, bour-geois multi-racialism.

These are some of the chief factors that have led to the black attack on multi-racialism and the emergence of Black Theology.

The Method of Black Theology

Black Theology is a situational theology. And the situation is that of the black man in South Africa. This is its chief distin-guishing characteristic.

The classical theological method of the West, under which most if not all of us have suffered, has been to make a thorough, detailed and academic study of the major sources of Christian doctrine in order, we are told, to explore God's self-revelation. Classically these sources have been the Bible, Tradition and Reason. Thus our theological curriculum has taken us through Biblical studies. We have studied content, problems of authorship, problems of date of writing; we have learned the techniques of historical, form and source criticism to tear the texts open. Alongside this we have battled through the history and doctrine of the early ecumenical councils and creeds, the Trinitarian and Christological debates of the third and fifth centuries, and on through Augustine, the Reformation, the Counter-Reformation, the Council of Trent, St Thomas Aquinas, Papal encyclicals and modern theologians. Then we have struggled through philosophy and ethics.

Finally, we have been sent out as 'qualified' priests to be the

'servants' of our people – the people whose real-life problems
we have scarcely considered while gaining all our heady in-
formation. In the main we have found ourselves to be irrelevant. Few, if any, of us have been able to translate our learning
into relevant and life-enabling action. But this inability is not
the sign of weak minds. Many brilliant German academic
theologians were unable to make theological judgments on and
thus Christian responses to the fascism of Hitler's Germany.
They were not fools, but few were able to come out of their
detached academic hothouses to grapple with pulsating human
problems. They wanted to be left in peace to continue their
research. And the people were without spiritual leaders.

Black Theology seeks to cut across this classically arid de-
tachment. It begins with people – specific people, in a specific
situation and with specific problems to face. Thus it starts
with black people in the South African situation facing the
strangling problems of oppression, fear, hunger, insult and
dehumanisation. It tries to understand as clearly as possible
who these people are, what their life experiences are, and the
nature and cause of their suffering. This is an indispensable
datum of Black Theology.

In asking the question 'What has happened to bring these
people to this situation?', two other questions will have to be
asked. First, where have these people come from?, i.e. what is
their African heritage? How was their society organised to
cope with starvation or healing before the arrival of the white
man? What was the nature of their faith and the character and
function of their religious life before the white man's God came
and condemned this faith and life as heathen and immoral?

Secondly, and closely related to the first question, they will
have to ask what has been the impact on black life of the arrival
of the white colonialists and their religion. This too is an indispensable datum of Black Theology.

Then Black Theology will be able to turn to the Scripture and
tradition. But it will turn to these classical sources of doctrine
not for their own sake, but to ask them what, if anything,
they have to say to these black people, with this history, in this
situation, facing these problems. It will ask of them 'Was our
black society and history and culture, before the white man
came, so rotten and heathen that it had to be destroyed?'

It will ask of them their judgment on the rich who oppress the poor? It will ask of them what hope they hold out for the oppressed poor, what freedom means, and what the poor must do to throw off their chains?

To put it differently in order to draw out the more practical inplications, I have often wondered what a white clergyman with a middle-class white suburban congregation would have to say to a black ghetto congregation in Soweto:* a people living illegally in the city, fearing the police, out of work, starving, cold and hungry, watching their babies die of malnutrition. 'Jesus loves you, love your neighbour'? Uneducated and unaware of world history and geography, as they invariably will be, what sense will they be able to make of his seminary image of Jesus of Nazareth. Where is Nazareth? What meaning would 'Son of Man', 'Messiah', 'Son of God', and so forth, convey? And if our white clergymen would be lost in this situation, so also are our white-trained, seminary hot-house black priests.

Some Content of Black Theology
What we have said on the method of Black Theology in South Africa must not be taken to imply that black theologians are free to make what they will of the sources of Christian doctrine (this allegation could be made with much more telling force against Oxford theology dons and German professors). The sources are important and relevant in so far as they are able to speak to us in our situation. Knowing the situation of blacks in South Africa, it is also important to know out of what sort of context the Biblical sources, for example, come. It is important and relvant to know that the Jews came into the land of Israel not as an imperialist army, but as a bunch of run-away slaves. It is important also to know that Jesus lived and taught in colonised Israel not as one of the Roman conquering group, but as one of the conquered Jews. It is therefore to be expected that an oppressed people should be able to turn to this sort of religious source with an air of expectant hope. And they have no need whatsoever to be guided by white Christianity or the white-dominated churches, for it must seem strange indeed that the religious literature of an oppressed people has given rise to a church, a theology and an ecclesiastical structure so

* A large African township near Johannesburg.

closely allied to the patterns of racist oppression in South Africa.

It is in the light of such considerations as these that Black
Theology's assertion that 'Christ is Black' needs to be assessed.
It is not a rush of hot religious emotionalism that has obscured
reason. At one level this assertion refers to the social fact that
it is the black people in South Africa who are the poor, the
colonised, the exploited, the oppressed, the discriminated-
against. Jesus as a Jew in first-century Israel was one of the
poor, the colonised, the oppressed. Through the incarnation
God identified himself in Christ with this group of people.
Thus a meaningful symbol of God's identification with the
oppressed is to say that Christ is black.

But there is also a second level of important meaning. Jesus
was no Roman Uncle Tom. Whatever his openness to the
Roman lackey tax-collectors, he was himself no tax-collector.
In fact at the beginning of his ministry he identifies his mission
as being 'to bring good news to the poor (he was poor); to proclaim liberty to captives (he too was a captive), and to the
blind new sight; to let the oppressed go free (he was a Jew
under Roman oppression); to proclaim the Lord's year of
favour' (Luke 4: 18). In other words Jesus was, though oppressed, a liberator of the oppressed. Belonging to the oppressed,
Christ is black. But he cannot be a black Uncle Tom. Christ
is Black (with a capital B), i.e. the one who is identified with
the blacks but stands amongst us as the Black liberator of the
blacks. Is not this image much closer to the red-blooded Jewish
Messiah, Jesus, than our pale and bloodless Jesus exhorting
us to love our neighbour by serving at a soup-kitchen?

This indicates clearly that the passionate concern of Black
Theology is with Liberation, with Freedom. It is natural therefore that it will explore new images of God. Blacks know what
it is to be the playthings of people in power and to be caught
at the suffering end of forces beyond their control. Concepts
such as omnipotence and omniscience ring fearfully of the
immoveable, military-backed South African government and
its Special Branch. These, however, are the images learned
from Western theology, and their biblical justification is dubi-
ous. Black Theology cannot afford to have any truck with these
images which lend religious support to a fascist type of authoritarianism. Nor should it lend ear to the pious clap-trap which

asserts that man cannot be free, he can only choose whose slave he will be – Christ's or the state's. It is slavery that is abhorrent, regardless of whether the slave master is kind or unkind.

The black man knows also what the white man's arrival has done to black society itself. The white man arrived with a concept of authority in which the man at the top of the pile was the one in whom decision-making was invested. The ordinary man was expected simply to obey or be punished. The white man naturally assumed that this too was the way authority functioned in black society. So he took tribal chiefs and turned them into white-style 'chief ministers' with a decision-making cabinet. It seems that they were unable to understand that in much black society, as in Biblical Israel, the chief or king had no authority over his people, but was rather the 'representative' or 'embodiment' of his people. His role was not decision-making. Decisions instead of starting at the 'top' to filter down through society, started at the 'bottom', filtering up through the various strata of society to be gathered together and unified in the wise chief. In African society 'authority' sprang out of the unity and well-being of the people. It was not the exercise of power over them.

The black man knows also that to talk about being human is to talk about humanising relationships; it is not to talk about the sheer brute fact of his physical existence. Talk about being human is not talk about biology or physiology. It is other people's attitudes to and relationships with us that enable us to walk tall and free. It is other people's patronising, insulting, disregarding, oppressing relationships with us that make us shrivel into nothings – often nothings even in our own eyes.

Thus Black Theology needs to explore images of God which are not sickening reflections of the white man's power-mad authoritarianism. We need new images which are freeing images in that they are images of unity and wholeness, images of humanising relationships of love and truth and justice and kindness and mercy. We will therefore assert that our image of God is of one who is enmeshed in the fabric of unity and wholeness, love and justice. God is no authoritarian king issuing commandments and rewarding or punishing according to our obedience or disobedience. Rather, God is discovered and known in the search for and experience of liberation, which is the wholeness of human life found only in the unity of liberating, life-affirming and dignifying relationships.

An appropriate symbol of this understanding of God would be that 'God is Freedom' – the freedom which has been revealed in our history, the freedom which we do experience despite all our chains, and the freedom that calls us forward infinitely to new and unexplored depths.

What then is this theology's concept of man? Man is he who is so inspired by the call of Freedom to a wholeness of life, and who loves himself and his fellows enough to be prepared to die rather than to give up the struggle to throw off the chains of slavery, oppression, poverty and authoritarianism.

Thus Black Theology is a passionate call to action for freedom, for God, for wholeness, for man.

2

BLACKNESS VERSUS NIHILISM: BLACK RACISM REJECTED

by Adam Small

Whites have for so long been dominant in South Africa – and in other parts of the world – that it is difficult for us who have partly *come* to recognise and partly been *forced* to recognise that indeed we are *not* white, to get those fellow-men of ours who also are indeed *not* white, but who have not yet recognised the facts to share this recognition with us. The reason why they have not yet come to this recognition that they are *not* white is that they still look upon White as an equivalent concept with Value. This is what the dominance of whites has done to the psychology of those fellowmen of ours. It has sapped their will and made them sluggish and indeed unwilling to draw themselves away from Whiteness, for that to them would mean to draw themselves away from Valuableness. Their equation of Whiteness with Valuableness is foolish and indeed dangerous for them, as it will destroy them.

I am writing of course of all those people, fellow-men of ours, who should be black and may I say that in this South African context I include under this term people of all shades of colour who are not considered by the laws and the people of this country to be white-people with black, brown and yellow skins. When I was invited to speak here, I was invited as a black, and immediately made a point of this. I was not invited as a non-black in the way that I used to be and still am invited, as a non-white. This form of the invitation in itself carries a profound meaning, and I ask all those present with us to ponder it. In itself it is a pointer to the fact that whites in South Africa already have to contend with a consciousness which no longer cares to define itself in terms of their whiteness and, moreover, negatively in terms of their whiteness.

We have come, and we are coming, to recognise ourselves as black, and at least a part of our task is, and will be, to unfetter every man who is not white from whiteness, that is from a misguided and dangerous belief in the equation I have mentioned. You will notice that I refer here to every man who is not white rather than to every man who is black; for it would be false to think that every man who is not white is, through that fact, black. This blackness of which we speak is certainly, amongst other things, a matter of 'the colour of the skin', however, as such it is something to which not we, but whites have first drawn attention, and we have no intention of defining ourselves basically in terms of anything that whites have marked out, or still mark out, for us. Therefore it is not in terms of skin colour that we see our blackness; it is a *certain awareness*, a certain insight.

It is important that we stress this fact because we find ourselves in South Africa where whites are present to an extent not found in the rest of our continent, and where we *do* have, and always will have, and always *must* have ties with whites in ways which our fellows elsewhere in the continent do not and cannot have. In speaking of our blackness as a certain awareness and insight, and in recognising that we are speaking thus in South Africa, we are at once identifying ourselves with blackness in the world at large and making emphases which are and must be unique for us.

That we do not make colour of the skin the basic criterion for our blackness must be evidence that this blackness is not racist. We have suffered enough from white racism not to want to be racist in our blackness. As I identify this blackness, our rejection of racism will become clear. Racism is a phenomenon of inferiority, whereas our blackness is a phenomenon of pride. We are not out to hate whites, but to treat them as people. Indeed in our blackness we can accommodate a sympathy for whites, which matches the sentiments of the black American writer who writes to his young nephew: 'There is no reason for you to try to become like white people and there is no basis whatever for their impertinent assumption that *they* must accept you. The really terrible thing, old buddy, is that *you* must accept *them*. . . . You must accept, and accept them with love. For these innocent people have no other hope.' We differ from this black writer only in that we do not believe these people to be innocent – perhaps he meant this only ironically.

It will be hard, this attempt to 'accept them with love'. For the natural thing for us as a result of white racism, whether crude or sugar-coated, is not to 'accept them with love' but to reject them with hatred. The things they have done to us need no repetition – we have named them often enough, and protested often enough without being understood, whether willfully or through ignorance. They 'know' us, they are even 'experts' on us, but they don't understand. After all, we still sing and we still dance. The words of Langston Hughes, the black poet, are apt for our situation too:

Because my mouth
is wide with laughter
and my throat
is deep with song,
you do not think
I suffer after
I have held my pain
so long.
Because my mouth
is wide with laughter
you do not hear
my inner cry;
Because my feet
are gay with dancing,
you do not know
I die.

The point, however, is that we can no longer care whether or not whites understand us. What we do care about is understanding ourselves and, in the course of this task, helping whites to understand themselves – in the words of the black author I have already quoted, helping them 'to see themselves as they are, to cease fleeing from reality'.

We can see that this insistence upon ourselves, this new turning away from the white world towards ourselves, is not passing unnoticed by whites; they have written about it in their newspapers, where they say it is to be feared. We say to them, however, that they have something worse to fear: themselves. We are cutting ourselves loose from their ideas of us, and of course this disturbance is terrible for whites. As our author says, 'the black man has functioned in the white man's world as a fixed star, as an immovable pillar: and as he moves out of his place, heaven and earth are shaken to their foundation.' To his nephew, again, he writes: 'I said that it was intended that you should perish in the ghetto, perish by never being allowed to go behind the white man's definitions, by never recognising that we are black in senses we give to blackness instead of senses they give to blackness. . . . These people who believed that your imprisonment made them safe are losing their grasp of reality.' Whites ought to fear this more than anything else; perhaps it is too accommodating to speak of a *loss* of grasp, for insofar as they have always thought wrongly about blackness, they never have had a grasp on reality. But then we too are only now beginning to think properly about blackness.

Through our turning towards our blackness, we wish to help whites to understand themselves and grasp a reality in which blackness occurs – and looms large. In making this point we are innocent of racism, for racism desires apartheid, which we reject as alienation, a philosophy of enmity.

I must define our blackness briefly, and as an introduction I quote the following beautiful lines from a young black American woman poet, Desirée Barnwell:

> Will the real black people please stand:
> Those fearless of the unconventional,
> Moved towards their own blackness,
> Prone to influence and set trends,
> Schooled in *their* times and folkways,
> Dedicated to worthwhile endeavours,
> Attentive to meaningful expression.

The real people in South Africa are those who reject definition of themselves in the clichéd categories of white 'race relations' parlance. The real *black* people are those who embrace the positive description 'black' as opposed to 'non-white' which is a definition in terms of others, not of oneself. The 'real black people' are 'moved towards their own blackness'. It is a matter of not running away from oneself, but daring to come face to face with oneself. Have whites – in South Africa at least – ever dared to do this? There has never been a situation which forces this upon them – not until now. The very situation which now makes us look at ourselves now does the same for them for the first time in world history. We want to face up to our blackness and all its consequences. Do whites, however, want to face up to their whiteness and all its consequences, even now? We have said that we wish to help them, and we can do so from our position of blackness; and we are in a much better position to help them than they are to help us.

We will live without apology, or as if apologising. Why, and to whom, must we apologise, or live as if we apologise, for being ourselves? We cannot apologise for being ourselves; we will live autonomously as ourselves. Whoever thinks this a trivial statement does not know the extent to which whites have goaded and do goad us to humiliations which all add up to our believing that we live by their grace. Now we are rejecting the idea – their idea, which unfortunately has also become deeply embedded in the souls of many of us – that we live even to the least degree by their grace. We may live by the grace of God, but we do not live by the grace of whites. This idea that they hold life for us in their hands has been the biggest impertinence on the part of whites. This has been the idea of even the 'best and most liberal' of whites – those who have wanted to give us this life which they believe they hold in their hands for us, quite freely or reasonably freely.

Our movement towards our blackness means the clear realisation that no one at all holds life for us in his hands. We are not beggars for life. We all live in this world, black and white. The meaning of this is something we will try to let whites see, and understand. This is one of the meanings of trying to help them to grasp reality.

Protest will therefore play a role in our future actions, but we will realise that protest is a kind of begging, and we cannot beg. Protests will be a secondary form of expression for us. Our primary form of expression will be the repeated manifestation of our blackness, time and time again. Whether or not whites understand this will be beside the point.

It must be clear for anyone who knows the meaning of

culture that blackness is for us a supremely cultural fact. It is, in this South African context, the consciousness that we have tremendous resources of the soul at our disposal out of which to grow strong in every sense, as long as we can succeed in eliminating the white man's ideas about us from our minds, if we can kill in ourselves the ridiculous equation of the white with the valuable. We do not say that blackness is *also* valuable – that would be to revert to seeing ourselves in terms of whiteness. Only values are valuable; we have values and we will work with them. Protagonists of apartheid – but also white antagonists of apartheid – love to cast themselves in the role of our guardians and approach us as little children, telling us 'You too have beautiful values, can't you see?' We in our blackness despise and laugh at these people.

Our blackness, in other words, is a consciousness of our own worth which flies in the face of every white approach to us that we know. In America, writes Addison Gayle, there are many white 'experts' on black 'subjects', from Harriet Beecher Stowe to Norman Mailer, and of course South Africa has its white experts on us. Whites know and approach us from the outside; even where their intentions are as pure as possible, they are on the outside. From the inside we know them well enough. The non-privileged of a society always know the privileged of that society better than the other way round. Our blackness will therefore appear strange to whites in any case. But the way we will stand in our blackness now, the autonomous unapologising way, the *proud* way – this they will find incomprehensible. We can help them to understand. However, our first task will be simply to live our blackness on every front. Culture is a comprehensive phenomenon: on all fronts we will be discovering our worth, the worth that whites cannot be truly concerned about because, however well-motivated they may be, they cannot penetrate to it – at least not yet. At this stage of the world's history nihilism, as Nietzsche saw it – that it is sheer self-interest – sits fast in the breast of every white man, even despite himself; his position in relation to the black man is defined nihilistically.

Our blackness – black consciousness – is not a matter of severing contacts so much as it is a matter of a certain historical necessity. Whites are fond of speaking of survival. They may begin to understand blackness a little if they think that blacks too have a will to survive the fury of our time.

If therefore we reject apartheid it is for a much profounder reason than that we want *integration*; for we do not want integration, we reject it. We want to survive as men, and if we do not insist on our blackness we are not going to make it in a world generously peopled with white nihilists, and especially not in a part of the world where we have to live with them, close to them, even in their midst.

3

THE CONCEPT OF GOD IN BLACK THEOLOGY

by Sabelo Ntwasa and Basil Moore

Introduction

This paper will suffer from two major omissions. The first
is that it will not attempt to deal with the concept of God in
traditional African religions in Southern Africa. Such a study
has been omitted, despite its importance, because it is a major
study on its own. Secondly, this paper will not attempt to
summarise the major concepts of God presented in Black
Theology by theologians overseas. This again is a major study
on its own.

Our method of approach will be, first to examine the predominating concepts of God which black people in South
Africa have learned from white missionaries and theological
teachers and which are the current 'orthodox' concepts of
God in the minds of most black (and white) Christians;
secondly, to look at the situation of black people in South
Africa and the implications of these images in this situation;
and thirdly, in the light of these considerations we shall explore the possibility of new images which are more situationally
relevant but not anti-Christian.

(i) The Predominating Christian Concepts of God

At the outset it needs to be acknowledged that we shall be
talking in generalisations which may at times seem to be
caricatures because we shall take into account neither all the
niceties of Western concepts of God nor the exceptions among
some Western theologians. At the same time the intention is

not to caricature but to present generalisations which are sufficiently accurate and wide-ranging to require a serious response.

(*a*) *God is a Person.* This is perhaps the major image of God in Western theology, so deeply embedded in our religious language and consciousness that when alternative images are presented such as Tillich's image of God as the 'ground and power of being', the level of reaction is feverishly emotional (cf. the debate on John Robinson's *Honest to God*).

This primary image is the basis for the more secondary image of God as 'Father', 'Son', 'Holy Spirit', etc.; whatever may have been meant by the Latin *persona* and Greek *prosopa* in the original credal definitions, the English word 'Person' has specific connotations. It is thesc English connotations which we build into the image of God as a 'Person'.

The normal anthropomorphic connotations of the 'Person' image of God are reinforced in the various artistic representations of God. In pictorial art God is usually depicted as a somewhat rarified human being. This is particularly true of Christ, who takes on the unmistakeable racial and fashion characteristics of the people involved (usually he is a medieval European). In dramatic art God's physical 'person' is not usually portrayed. But if he 'speaks', the voice is usually unmistakably human and male.

Despite acknowledgements of the inadequacies and dangers of anthropomorphism, the tenacity of the 'Person' image has been remarkable. Thus in the Trinitarian debates of the third century the 'Person' image created enormous problems in asserting God's transcendence, his immanence and his unity. The transcendent God (the Father) is a 'Person'. So also is the immanent God (the Son). So we have two 'Persons', and the tortuous course of the debate was to find a way of making the two 'Persons' one 'Person'. Time and again the 'Person' image collapsed under the strain. But if the image collapsed or was scrapped by the struggling theologian of the period, he was usually thrown out as a heretic. The image was regarded as so fundamental that men were killed for questioning it. It has remained so fundamental that one has to ask whether it has not become an idol.

But it is not so much the 'Person' symbol that has been crucial in the development of Western theology and Christianity as the secondary images which have been allied to it.

(*b*) *God is the Omnipotent, Omniscient, Supreme Authority.* Perhaps it is God's 'supreme authority' which is the most important in this trilogy of Divine attributes. The story of Adam and Eve in the second creation story brings out this absolute and unquestionable authority of God most clearly. God is presented in the story as placing a total prohibition on consuming the fruit of the tree of 'the knowledge of good and evil' and the tree of 'life'. The fruit of any other trees is available to the man (Adam). No reasons whatever are given for these prohibitions. Man is simply to obey because God has so commanded. Exegetes have given many fine explanations of this demand, but the over-riding impression is that God has the right to make demands of total obedience of men.

In the story this demand for unquestioning obedience then runs on into God's omnipotence. Not only is God the creator, but he also has the power to punish the disobedient and reward the obedient. The demand for obedience is accompanied by a solemn warning that disobedience will be punished by 'death', and the story closes on the punishment meted out to Adam, Eve and the serpent when they disobey the Divine command.

If God is omnipotent, he is also omniscient. No man can hide his disobedience from God. God always knows, as he knew Adam's sin. There is simply no escape for man from the all-seeing, all-knowing and all-powerful God.

The concept of the absolute authority, all-knowing and all-powerful God pervades our Christian language. The words used to describe the human relationship to God are 'surrender', 'obedience', 'letting God take complete control', 'acceptence', etc. It is not unknown for Christian preachers to present 'God's demands', linked closely with 'God's power and omniscience', in a form of fear-inducing threats. 'Hell' will be the inevitable consequence for those who disobey, and 'Heaven' the sublime reward of the obedient. People are, in effect, bullied (though the preachers would call it 'exhorted') into submitting to God's demands.

(*c*) *God is a White Male.* When the 'Person' symbol of God is accepted, together with his trilogy of attributes as omnipotent, omniscient and absolute authority, the inescapable impression is of a super-human tyrant ruler over man, who is however beneficent to his obedient slaves. On to this 'super-being' image further secondary but equally devaating anthropomorphisms become attached.

The first of these is that God is not simply the supreme authority but that God is male. Invariably in the Bible God is of the male gender, 'He'. This is true even in Greek and Hebrew. 'God' and 'Lord' (Hebrew *elohim* and *adonai* and Greek *theos* and *kurios*) are masculine nouns. In English it is difficult indeed to imagine using any pronoun other than 'He' when speaking of God. As we have already seen when God is artistically represented, it is undoubtedly a male figure or voice.

Corresponding to the maleness of God there is a striking amount of anti-feminism in the Bible (e.g. St Paul's dictum that women are to remain silent in the assemblies of the congregation), in sophisticated theological writings (e.g. Karl Barth's claim that women are 'ontologically inferior' to men), and ecclesiastical structures (have there been any women popes, cardinals, bishops or priests? How many denominations are prepared to ordain women to the clergy and for how long have they been prepared to do so?).

In his 'Person', sex (male) is invariably attributed to God. Since the all-powerful, all-knowing, supreme authority is male, women have almost invariably been excluded from positions of authority, if not excluded as persons from the human race and thus subjected to indignities, insults and oppression.

Just as the 'Person' symbol attracts a sexual image, so it attracts a racial image. Despite all the theological disclaimers about God's non-racial identity, Western theology and art have made him supremely 'white'. It is only very recently that a few African artists have dared to allow God or Christ to be black. All the classical portrayals of God in art are of a white male. It is only very recently also that a few Black theologians have dared to symbolise God or Christ as black. Not many reputable theologians would have echoed Barth's human ontology and claimed that 'whites are ontologically superior', but there is no doubt that racist theologians have made this sort of claim in different ways.

In South Africa the Christian God's whiteness has been there from the beginning, if not always overtly. The strange white man arrived on our soil with his strange new God, and set himself up as the ecclesiastical authority – a position he has never relinquished. And this white man in his zeal condemned everything in black religion and culture as 'heathen' and 'immoral'. 'Conversion' entailed breaking with Africa and taking on Europe in dress, faith, education, medicine, farming, marriage and tribal life. It was inevitable, therefore, that the 'converts' would link the alien God with the alien missionaries and the alienating new life-style demanded of them. The whole was 'white', including God.

Allied with this whiteness was the new pattern of authority which came with the colonising bed-fellows of the missionaries. Before the arrival of the white colonists in Southern Africa, decision-making mostly did not rest in the hands of the chief who ruled over his people. The chief, rather, gathered together and embodied the decisions which began 'at the bottom' and filtered painstakingly 'up' through a series of *indabas*. More crucial than speed and 'efficiency' was the well-being and contentment of the tribal unit. With the colonists came a form of authority in which decision-making rested in the hands of the man 'at the top', the white governor, with a police force to ensure that his laws were obeyed. This new political pattern was also the pattern in the new religion, which sought justification in affirming God as the supreme authority even over the ecclesiastical authorities. This new pattern further reinforced the 'whiteness' of this strange God.

When Black theologians like James Cone attempt to cut across this 'whiteness' of God to affirm his 'blackness' they do little to cut across the more fundamental issues in the image of God as 'Person' with his trilogy of absolute power attributes. As victims of their colonial past they speak a word of hope to blacks in their struggle against whites, but they say little that is filled with hope to blacks as people. What difference does the colour of a tyrant make? Are whites alone capable of being fascists?

There are many other attributes of God in traditional Western theology which we ought to consider, but most of them reinforce in different ways the images already considered. Thus the symbol of God as 'Father' reinforces his maleness and authority; God as 'Son' reinforces his maleness; God as 'Shepherd' or 'Guide' or 'Lord' or 'King' or 'Master' reinforces his authority; even God as 'servant', like God as 'Father', while attempting to express God's loving concern, still carries strong overtones of authority. (Thus we frequently say that a Bishop is to be the servant of his people!)

(ii) The Situation of Black People in South Africa in the Perspective of these Symbols of God

We have already tried to show that while the image of God as 'Person' is the primary image in Western Christian theology, the other attributes which it attracts to itself, i.e. the images of the relations of this 'Person' with man, are crucial. Thus it would be more meaningful and profitable to return to the 'Person' symbol after considering the others.

(a) *God as the Omnipotent, Omniscient, Supreme Authority.* In South Africa the black man knows and feels the crunch of his suffering at the point of his blackness. He is completely justified, therefore, in claiming that he is suffering because of his blackness. But he is mistaken if he sees his exclusion from social, political and religious affairs and decision-making as nothing other than the result of white racism. Racism is important, but only as a powerful emotional factor bolstering the desire of a minority of the people to keep effective power entirely within their own hands. Our white rulers build up and then rely on the racial prejudices of the white people to return them to office with ever-increasing dictatorial powers. It is the underlying authoritarianism which is sick and felt by the black man in its racist manifestation (it would be felt by the white man also if only he would take time to think).

The black man in South Africa possibly knows better than any other man what it is to be under a de-humanising authority. He is excluded from making the most basic decisions that affect his own life – where he will find shelter; where and what and how he will work for his food and drink; how he will organise his life together with others. All these sorts of decisions are made for him; he has simply to obey. And the decisions that are made for him are seldom, if ever, the decisions he would have made for himself, for they are decisions made always in favour of the white man. He will live in over-crowded hovels or on over-populated land as far removed as possible from white-owned places of employment (the only employment available to most blacks). He will do only poorly paid unskilled work, unless he can afford the education which will put him in one of the few available professions. No adequate provision is made if he or his children are sick.

The black man knows also that authoritarianism cannot work unless it is bolstered by a mass of physical might which also keeps a close watch on his thoughts, words and deeds. So he lives in a world where he knows that he can seldom escape the unsleeping eye and ear of the informer or security police. His is a world also populated with white soldiers, saracens, police dogs, policemen. If he does not obey the decisions made by an authority far beyond his influence he knows that he will be locked in prison, banned, house arrested, or will simply 'disappear'.

In this situation the Western images of God's absolute authority, power and knowledge are too distressingly familiar for comfort. In this situation too, Western theological authoritarianism provides a tremendous support for the *status quo*. Too many of our tyrants appeal to their 'hot line' of communication with God to justify their tyranny. If this is a twisted application of God's 'authority', it is to be expected. The black man must reject the pious nonsense that man cannot be free, he can only choose whose slave he will be. It is irrelevent whether the Master is kind or unkind. It is slavery he rejects and thus anything which lends respectability to slavery – especially religious respectability. And he rejects it because he knows the agony of being a slave whether his slavery has been experienced from the perspective of a migrant labourer or a professional lawyer. What is de-humanising is to have to put your life into the hands of another.

(*b*) *God as White.* In South Africa the black man's burden is the white man's authoritarianism, which erupts also in racism. It is also the devastating effect which this has had on his own pride in himself. Too many blacks have been beaten in every conceivable way until they have come to see themselves through the white man's eyes. Black is evil, dark, secret and reeking of 'witchcraft'. Black culture and religion are heathen and immoral. Black people are inferior, stupid, untrustworthy, cowardly, cringing.

In this situation Black theologians have to be iconoclasts of the 'white' God. They have to tear down every image and symbol which, by presenting God as 'white', reinforces this sense of human inferiority and worthlessness. This means not only removing 'white God' pictures, but more important, the white men who seem to believe that it is their whiteness that places them closer to God and thus to the source of the truth and ability.

(c) *God is Male.* If ever there are people who suffer under a double yoke it is South Africa's black women. Not only do they know what it is to be oppressed as blacks, an oppression they share with all blacks and which is a crippling enough burden; they also know what it is to be oppressed as women.

If black women are white men's nobodies (except the sex-objects of a few Nationalist perverts) they are also black men's property bought at a *lobola* price, and expected to be their obedient servants in the home. And if the black home is too poor to afford the luxury of a 'kitchen-servant' wife, then she must become the 'kitchen slave' of a white woman. An unmarried black woman knows fears and insecurities beyond those of her married black neighbours. In the cities she may not rent a house for herself, a right accorded to men only.

In the struggle for education in South Africa girls are given minor consideration. If a family is wealthy enough, girls may receive high school and university education, but if it is not, boys will always receive priority, irrespective of ability. This is to be expected since, as in white society, men always receive preference in employment, both in terms of being employed and in terms of salaries.

And if blacks generally have been kept out of leadership in the Church, black women have not even been considered, except in one or two isolated instances. Women are excluded as surely in the black churches as in the white-dominated ones.

Decision-making authority is primarily a white male privilege. Where a few chinks have appeared in white authority no significant one has opened up in male authority.

Black Theology, as it struggles to formulate a theology of liberation relevant to South Africa, cannot afford to perpetuate any form of domination, not even male domination. If its liberation is not human enough to include the liberation of women, it will not be liberation.

(*d*) *God as 'Person'.* We have argued that being a person is not being a brute physical object of the species *homo sapiens*. Talk about humanity cannot be taken simply as biological. It is rather, about relationships.

My being as a person is locked in with yours. I cannot be a person fully and completely in isolation. It does not matter how much the Bible or any other source affirms my worth as a human being. I only *feel* my worth when it is affirmed and not denied in inter-personal relationships.

The absurdity of the black man's existence is experienced when, on the one hand, formal religious language affirms his human worth as a creature, while on the other, secular and ecclesiastical practice denies it consistently and persistently. 'You are of infinite value to God', religious language proclaims. Life proclaims: 'I hope you will be satisfied with the value God places on you, because in our eyes you have none.'

Perhaps the image that best explains what is struggling to be said here is that humanity exists in the spaces between people, i.e. in the relationships that bind them together, that are mutually affirming, that are liberating and that create a wholeness. It is our relationships with each other springing from an authentic well within ourselves, that either build up (love) or break down (authoritarian prejudice).

Black Theology is as irrelvant as any other theology if it is not about human liberation, and thus about black liberation. It must therefore explore new symbols of God which affirm human authenticity, freedom and wholeness. The old images of God as 'Person', 'over' or 'beyond' us, will no longer do. Authentic wholeness will come only as we are bound together in our affirmation of each other. It certainly has not come through common allegiance to persons, states, countries or Gods.

(*iii*) *Relational Symbols of God*

Traditional Christianity has always asserted God's transcendence and his immanence, the images of which have been of a great Father-figure 'out there' and a loving Son 'amongst us'. For the reasons already given, these symbols must be rejected.

If true humanness – and hence freedom and wholeness – lies in the spaces between people, and if God is about true humanness and thus freedom and wholeness, we need new images of God which give content and direction to the 'spaces between people', i.e. we need relational images of God.

If, for example, we say with St John that 'God is love' and take this literally rather than figuratively (i.e. God is a 'Person' who 'loves me'), then it is possible to conceive transcendence and immanence in new ways. We know something of immanent love in our own experience, and learn its meaning more deeply as we explore our history. At every point where love is known and felt and shown, there God is experienced and revealed to us, in us, and through us. Some men know and show love fleetingly and imperfectly. Others, like Christ, are burning, glowing incarnations of it. But despite all we know, have learned and have experienced of love, we know that we have not yet experienced it in all its fullness. We know nothing of how a totally loving and life-affirming society would be. There is, we believe and hope, always a 'beyond' to love. This 'beyond' (call it transcendence if it helps) calls us forward to bold new ventures.

Thus there is the known, the experienced, the immanent in the personal relationships of love, but there is also the unknown, the not-yet-experienced, the transcendent. And if anyone tells us that love is nothing but an abstract construct without power, we can only reply that he has not yet begun to live.

But in exploring a new relational image of God we need something more total and more vital than the much-abused 'love'. Perhaps such an image would be 'God is Freedom'. God is the freedom made known in our history. God is the freedom fleetingly and incompletely known in our own experience. But God is also the freedom beyond anything we have yet known, the freedom that calls us out of our chains of oppression into a wholeness of life. God is this wholeness which exists in the spaces between the people when their dignity and worth is mutually affirmed in love, truth, honesty, justice and caring warmth.

If we were attempting to depict God understood in this new

symbol of Freedom that means wholeness, we would take seriously the old Hebrew dictum that God cannot be represented in any created object. But we would depict people in love, or people throwing off their shackles of slavery, or people raising their fists aloft in a call and salute to freedom.

The old Negro spiritual sings our new hymn well:

Oh Freedom, oh Freedom,
Oh Freedom over me.
And before I'll be a slave
I'll be buried in my grave,
and go home to my Lord and be free.

4

AN AFRICAN THEOLOGY OR
A BLACK THEOLOGY

by Manas Buthelezi

No one who is seriously concerned about the future of Christianity in South Africa can afford to ignore the current quest for a Black Theology, regardless of whether this phenomenon has been adequately defined or not. No serious minister who deserves the faithful allegiance of a self-respecting black man can for a moment doubt the legitimacy of the quest for a theological assessment of the incarnation of the Word of God in the peculiarities of the life and thought processes of the black people of South Africa.

I am not by any means an accredited spokesman for the so called Black Theology movement. Yet, I belong to the anthropological and sociological medium out of which the quest for a Black Theology has emerged. We should not get bogged down in questions of academic sophistry and semantics, namely, whether theology can be black or white. This is a facetious way of pointing out that the meaning and significance of words, like that of symbols, derives from the intrinsic worth of the concept or reality they are understood to stand for.

The phrase 'Black Theology' comes out of an attempt to characterize by means of a word or phrase the reflection upon the reality of God and his Word which grows out of that experience of life in which the category of blackness has some existential decisiveness. I shall elaborate on this later.

To interpret the quest for a Black Theology purely in terms of the awakening of black nationalism or the consolidation of Black Power forces us to trifle with one of the most fundamental issues in modern Christianity. We know that this not uncommon appraisal of the phenomenon of the quest for a Black Theology is often expressed in pejorative phrases calculated to call in question the theological integrity of the quest itself. The indiscriminate alignment of Christian black awareness with an emotionally-charged political concept 'Black Power' is sometimes a deliberate campaign to malign even the black man's token attempt to understand and interpret himself as an unconditional human being. This impression is given even in certain church papers and news releases which is ironical.

In many international church conferences Younger Churches have been challenged to interpret the Gospel in the light of their indigenous life situations. John V. Taylor has summed up what this challenge involves:

> Christ has been presented as the answer to the questions a white man would ask, the solution to the needs that the Western man would feel, the Saviour of the world of the European worldview, the object of the adoration and prayer of historic Christendom. But if Christ were to appear as the answer to the questions that Africans are asking, what would he look like? If he came into the world of African cosmology to redeem Man as Africans understand him, would he be recognizable to the rest of the Church Universal? And if Africa offered him the praises and petitions of her total uninhibited humanity would they be acceptable?
>
> (*The Primal Vision*, London: SCM Press, 1963, p. 24)

These thought-provoking questions asked by Taylor point to the essence of the quest for a Black Theology or, to use a more established phrase, 'African' or 'indigenous' theology. In the past there was no clarity on what the protagonists for Indigenous Theology meant when they stated their case. As we all know, pertinent to what we mean by theology is the way we arrive at it, namely, theological method. In a sense, the phrase 'Black Theology' indicates a particular option of theological method *vis-à-vis* so called 'African Theology'. It is this distinction which I wish to delineate. The hope is that we shall thus arrive at an understanding of 'Black Theology'.

It is possible to distinguish two approaches to indigenous theology in South Africa: the ethnographic and the anthropological. The distinction centres on whether the point of departure in our theological method should be an ethnographic reconstruction of the African past or a dialogue with the present-day anthropological realities in South Africa.

(i) *Ethnographic Approach*

As the name indicates the point of departure here is the finding of ethnography. It is in place to explain first what we mean in this context by ethnography. According to A. L. Kroeber, 'by usage rather than definition, ethnography deals with the cultures of non-literate peoples. Unlike history, which deals with written documents, ethnography does not find its documents; it makes them by direct experience of living or by interview, question and record.'

As elements of literature, concepts like 'the African mind', the 'African world-view', etc., exist mainly as ethnographic reconstructions. I am fond of quoting Tempels to illustrate this point. Placide Tempels in his *Bantu Philosophy* has stated that the Bantu are not capable of articulating that which is latent in them by formulating a philosophical treatise which is complete with an adequate vocabulary. Hence 'it is our job', says Tempels, 'to proceed to such systematic development. It is we who will be able to tell them, in precise terms, what their inmost concept of being is. They will recognise themselves in our words and will acquiesce, saying, You understand us: you "know" in the way we "know"'.

In a different context Bengt Sundkler states that the African theologian must use as his point of departure the fundamental facts in terms of which the African interprets existence and the universe. African theology must take account of the myths of the African religion, which may serve as a good conceptual frame of reference. 'The myths span the whole of existence, from heaven to the hut and the heart of the individual; in fact, from cosmos to clan. Macrocosm and microcosm are tuned to each other and are included in an all-embracing order.'

I am not by any means calling in question the possibility and validity of an ethnographic reconstruction as such; what is rather at issue is the validity of an ethnographic reconstruction as a point of departure in the theological methodology. There are two disturbing features in this approach.

1. TENDENCY TOWARDS CULTURAL OBJECTIVISM

Too much emphasis is placed upon the African world-view as if it were an isolated and independent entity apart from the present anthropological reality of the African man. The quest for an indigenous theology seems to be understood as originating from the problem of a conflict between two world-views: the European and the African. The human factor seems to recede to the background, if recognised at all. It then becomes a problem of epistemological entities; of fixed impersonal data – things 'out there', namely, the body of categories for interpreting the universe. These categories are static entities which form something which can be located, studied and described – thanks to ethnography! Hence Tempels can confidently say what Europeans will be able to reveal to Africans.

2. TENDENCY TO OVERLOOK PRESENT-DAY REALITIES

Related to the above is the tendency to romanticise the ethnographically reconstructed historical past at the expense of the anthropological dynamics of the present situation. To be sure, the past can serve as an important instrument for inspiring man in his present-day responsibilities. Looking back to the past served as a catalyst in the lasting achievements of the Renaissance and Reformation movements.

Taylor has argued that the African world-view, which is at the same time inherent in and independent of the traditional religion, 'stands in the world as a living faith, whether in the residual paganism of millions, or in the tacit assumptions of very many African Christians, or the neo-African culture of the intellectual leaders.' True as this may be, we should not forget that there is a difference between psychologically living in the past in order to escape from the harsh realities of the present which one cannot face squarely at the moment, and living in the past because it can give the spiritual and physical bread for the day. It is too presumptuous to claim to know how much of his past the African will allow to shape his future, as soon as he is given the chance to participate in all that constitutes the wholeness of life at present.

It should be allowed that, even if the West had not impinged upon Africa, Africa could still have undergone a metamorphosis on her own under the impulse of her people's changing needs. Such internal changes could obviously not leave the old world-view unchanged.

For these reasons the 'ethnographic' approach to indigenous theology falls short. For theology to be indigenous, it is not enough that it should deal merely with 'African things' like the African world-view; it must also reflect the life dynamics of the present-day African.

(ii) *Anthropological Approach*

In the light of this approach the starting point for theological reflection is the existential situation in which the Gospel finds man. Just as one needs to take man's sinful state seriously in order to grasp the depth of the forgiving love of God, one must also take seriously the decisive factors that shape the mode of man's daily existence in order to see in perspective the direction as well as the ultimate fruition of the formation of the new man in Christ through the Word of God. The Word of God reaches man in his real situation, which may not always be an ideal one. In the Black Theology methodology we find an instance of the demonstration of this truth by means of theological reflection.

Let me begin by analysing the theological meaning of blackness. Blackness is a life category that embraces the totality of my daily existence. It determined the circumstances of my growth as a child and the life possibilities open to me. It now determines where I live, worship, minister and the range of my closest life associates. Can you think of a more decisive factor in life? The totality of the only life I know has unfolded itself to me within the limits and range of black situational possibilities. Whether or not anyone who observes my life may think that it is too special to be normal is immaterial; it is my only experience of life, and this fact determines the hermeneutical setting for the Word of God which is designed to save me within the context of my real situation.

As long as this homiletical and hermeneutical situation does not undergo outward and inward change, any genuine reflection on my encounter with the Word of God will necessarily be tainted with my experience of the reality of life. By the same token, any valid hermeneutical adaptation of the message of

God's Word for me will have to take into account the context
of my life situation.

To use more concrete expression, a man who has lived to
know other black men as his only everyday-life brothers cannot
have any faith in the church as a medium in which solidari-
ties according to the categories of blackness and whiteness have
been dissolved. A genuine theology grows out of the dynamic
forces in life, forces which are decisive for the shaping of everyday life. As far as I can judge, Black Theology is nothing but a
methodological formula whose genius consists in paying tribute
to the fact that theological honesty cannot but recognise the
peculiarity of the black man's situation. To be theologically
honest, one need not reconstruct first the situation in which our
grandfathers lived. The realisation of our authentic humanity
as black people does not consist merely in reconstructing the
old patterns of a past theological and sociological world-view,
but in gaining access as black people to that which constitutes
the wholeness of life in the present day world. Whatever lasting
spiritual insights the old world-view contained will be activated
only as we realise our humanity by meaningfully sharing in all
the life-facilities the present day world offers.

Pride in one's traditional heritage is the fruit of pride in
one's dignity as man. A self-despising man is ashamed of his
past as well as of anything that is related to him. Any proposal
that this man should go back to his traditional customs will
only serve to enslave his mind more, since he is not yet psychologically redeemed. I am suspicious of 'African experts' who,
without being invited, come from outside our black experience
and propose theological as well as sociological programmes
showing how the past cultural patterns can shape and condition our lives today. It must be a black man who knows how
best to live as a black man today.

A relevant message of the Gospel is that which not only
helps the black man to regain his self-confidence and respect
as a human being, but which focuses attention on the removal
of the dehumanising facets of modern life. For instance, people
who live in perpetual poverty and other humiliating life
circumstances will never fully understand what God intended
when he created them as men and redeemed them in Christ.
They will thus be missing one of the fundamental truths about

God's intended meaning of our present life. For them, the question 'Why did God create us?' will remain a perpetual puzzle and mental agony. For many people today, blackness is a life stigma from which they continually try to escape both psychologically and intellectually. That is why many Zulu-speaking black people switch over to broken and rotten Zulu when they address white people who fail to speak Zulu properly; Fanakalo* is a language which has flowered from the grave of the black man's dignity.

If the Gospel means anything, it must save the black man from his own blackness. It must answer his basic existential question 'Why did God create me black?' This problem has partly been accentuated by linguistic usage. In many languages blackness is a symbol of evil, sin and ugliness; it is also a symbol of death and mourning. If St John the Divine in the Book of Revelation describes the risen saints as dressed in white, he was merely following a certain language pattern and not some divinely inspired spiritual categories.   . .

The black man must be enabled through the interpretation and application of the Gospel to realise that blackness, like whiteness, is a good natural face cream from God and not some cosmological curse. Here lies the contribution of Black Theology's methodological technique. Black Theology challenges established Christianity to engage in a dialogue with the black people who feel that somehow theology has not taken them into consideration. It cautions the preacher and minister to stop preaching a 'pie in the sky' religion, but instead to come down and toil with the black man spiritually and existentially in the sweat and dust of daily life. As soon as this objective has been realised, the whole world will know us as human beings and not merely study-curiosities to adorn the pages of doctoral dissertations.

* A bastardised version of Zulu, with a very basic vocabulary, used as a means of communication (mainly instruction) in the South African mines.

5

BLACK CONSCIOUSNESS AND THE QUEST FOR A TRUE HUMANITY

by Steve Biko

It is perhaps fitting to start by examining why it is necessary for us to think collectively about a problem we never created. In doing so, I do not wish to concern myself unnecessarily with the white people of South Africa, but to get to the right answers, we must ask the right questions; we have to find out what went wrong – where and when; and we have to find out whether our position is a deliberate creation of God or an artificial fabrication of the truth by power-hungry people whose motive is authority, security, wealth and comfort. In other words, the 'Black Consciousness' approach would be irrelevant in a colourless and non-exploitative egalitarian society. It is relevant here because we believe that an anomalous situation is a deliberate creation of man.

There is no doubt that the colour question in South African politics was originally introduced for economic reasons. The leaders of the white community had to create some kind of barrier between blacks and whites so that the whites could enjoy privileges at the expense of blacks and still feel free to give a moral justification for the obvious exploitation that pricked even the hardest of white consciences. However, tradition has it that whenever a group of people has tasted the lovely fruits of wealth, security and prestige it begins to find it more comfortable to believe in the obvious lie and to accept it as normal that it alone is entitled to privilege. In order to believe this seriously, it needs to convince itself of all the arguments that support the lie. It is not surprising, therefore, that in South Africa, after generations of exploitation, white people on the whole have come to believe in the inferiority of the black man, so much so that while the race problem started as an offshoot of the economic greed exhibited by white people, it has now become a serious problem on its own. White people now despise black people, not because they need to reinforce their attitude and so justify their position of privilege but simply because they actually believe that black is inferior and bad. This is the basis upon which whites are working in South Africa, and it is what makes South African society racist.

The racism we meet does not only exist on an individual basis; it is also institutionalised to make it look like the South African way of life. Although of late there has been a feeble attempt to gloss over the overt racist elements in the system, it is still true that the system derives its nourishment from the existence of anti-black attitudes in society. To make the lie live even longer, blacks have to be denied any chance of accidentally proving their equality with white men. For this reason there is job reservation, lack of training in skilled work, and a tight orbit around professional possibilities for blacks. Stupidly enough, the system turns back to say that blacks are inferior because they have no economists, no engineers, etc., although it is made impossible for blacks to acquire these skills.

To give authenticity to their lie and to show the righteousness of their claim, whites have further worked out detailed schemes to 'solve' the racial situation in this country. Thus, a pseudo-parliament has been created for 'Coloureds',* and several 'Bantu states' are in the process of being set up. So independent and fortunate are they that they do not have to spend a cent on their defence because they have nothing to fear from white South Africa which will always come to their assistance in times of need. One does not, of course, fail to see the arrogance of whites and their contempt for blacks, even in their well-considered modern schemes for subjugation.

The overall success of the white power structure has been in managing to bind the whites together in defence of the *status quo*. By skillfully playing on that imaginary bogey – *swart gevaar*† – they have managed to convince even diehard liberals that there is something to fear in the idea of the black man assum-

* Persons of mixed race, mostly living in Cape Province.
† Black peril.

ing his rightful place at the helm of the South African ship. Thus after years of silence we are able to hear the familiar voice of Alan Paton saying, as far away as London: 'Perhaps apartheid is worth a try'. 'At whose expense, Dr. Paton?', asks an intelligent black journalist. Hence whites in general reinforce each other even though they allow some moderate disagreements on the details of subjugation schemes. There is no doubt that they do not question the validity of white values. They see nothing anomalous in the fact that they alone are arguing about the future of 17 million blacks – in a land which is the natural backyard of the black people. Any proposals for change emanating from the black world are viewed with great indignation. Even the so-called Opposition, the United Party, has the nerve to tell the Coloured people that they are asking for too much. A journalist from a liberal newspaper like *The Sunday Times* of Johannesburg describes a black student – who is only telling the truth – as a militant, impatient young man.

It is not enough for whites to be on the offensive. So immersed are they in prejudice that they do not believe that blacks can formulate their thoughts without white guidance and trusteeship. Thus, even those whites who see much wrong with the system make it their business to control the response of the blacks to the provocation. No one is suggesting that it is not the business of liberal whites to oppose what is wrong. However, it appears to us as too much of a coincidence that liberals – few as they are – should not only be determining the *modus operandi* of those blacks who oppose the system, but also leading it, in spite of their involvement in the system. To us it seems that their role spells out the totality of the white power structure – the fact that though whites are our problem, it is still other whites who want to tell us how to deal with that problem. They do so by dragging all sorts of red herrings across our paths. They tell us that the situation is a class struggle rather than a racial one. Let them go to van Tonder* in the Free State and tell him this. We believe we know what the problem is, and we will stick by our findings.

I want to go a little deeper in this discussion because it is time we killed this false political coalition between blacks and whites as long as it is set up on a wrong analysis of our situation.

* Derogatory reference to the average Afrikaans-speaking farmer.

I want to kill it for another reason – namely that it forms at present the greatest stumbling block to our unity. It dangles before freedom-hungry blacks promises of a great future for which no one in these groups seems to be working particularly hard.

The basic problem in South Africa has been analysed by liberal whites as being apartheid. They argue that in order to oppose it we have to form non-racial groups. Between these two extremes, they claim, lies the land of milk and honey for which we are working. The *thesis*, the *anti-thesis* and the *synthesis* have been mentioned by some great philosophers as the cardinal points around which any social revolution revolves. For the *liberals*, the *thesis* is apartheid, the *antithesis* is non-racialism, but the *synthesis* is very feebly defined. They want to tell the blacks that they see integration as the ideal solution. Black Consciousness defines the situation differently. The *thesis* is in fact a strong white racism and therefore, the *antithesis* to this must, *ipso facto*, be a strong solidarity amongst the blacks on whom this white racism seeks to prey. Out of these two situations we can therefore hope to reach some kind of balance – a true humanity where power politics will have no place. This analysis spells out the difference between the old and new approaches. The failure of the liberals is in the fact that their *antithesis* is already a watered-down version of the truth whose close proximity to the thesis will nullify the purported balance. This accounts for the failure of the Sprocas* commissions to make any real headway, for they are already looking for an 'alternative' acceptable to the white man. Everybody in the commissions knows what is right but all are looking for the most seemly way of dodging the responsibility of saying what is right.

It is much more important for blacks to see this difference than it is for whites. We must learn to accept that no group, however benevolent, can ever hand power to the vanquished on a plate. We must accept that the limits of tyrants are prescribed by the endurance of those whom they oppress. As long as we go to Whitey begging cap in hand for our own emancipation, we are giving him further sanction to continue with

* Study Project on Authority in an Apartheid Society. Set up by S.A. Council of Churches and Christian Institute in 1968.

his racist and oppressive system. We must realise that our situation is not a mistake on the part of whites but a deliberate act, and that no amount of moral lecturing will persuade the white man to 'correct' the situation. The system concedes nothing without demand, for it formulates its very method of operation on the basis that the ignorant will learn to know, the child will grow into an adult and therefore demands will begin to be made. It gears itself to resist demands in whatever way it sees fit. When you refuse to make these demands and choose to come to a round table to beg for your deliverance, you are asking for the contempt of those who have power over you. This is why we must reject the beggar tactics that are being forced on us by those who wish to appease our cruel masters. This is where the S.A.S.O. message and cry *'Black man, you are on your own!'* becomes relevant.

The concept of integration, whose virtues are often extolled in white liberal circles, is full of unquestioned assumptions that embrace white values. It is a concept long defined by whites and never examined by blacks. It is based on the assumption that all is well with the system apart from some degree of mismanagement by irrational conservatives at the top. Even the people who argue for integration often forget to veil it in its supposedly beautiful covering. They tell each other that, were it not for job reservation, there would be a beautiful market to exploit. They forget they are talking about people. They see blacks as additional levers to some complicated industrial machines. This is white man's integration – an integration based on exploitative values. It is an integration in which black will compete with black, using each other as rungs up a step ladder leading them to white values. It is an integration in which the black man will have to prove himself in terms of these values before meriting acceptance and ultimate assimilation, and in which the poor will grow poorer and the rich richer in a country where the poor have always been black. We do not want to be reminded that it is we, the indigenous people, who are poor and exploited in the land of our birth. These are concepts which the Black Consciousness approach wishes to eradicate from the black man's mind before our society is driven to chaos by irresponsible people from Coca-cola and hamburger cultural backgrounds.

Black Consciousness is an attitude of mind and a way of life, the most positive call to emanate from the black world for a long time. Its essence is the realisation by the black man of the need to rally together with his brothers around the cause of their oppression – the blackness of their skin – and to operate as a group to rid themselves of the shackles that bind them to perpetual servitude. It is based on a self-examination which has ultimately led them to believe that by seeking to run away from themselves and emulate the white man, they are insulting the intelligence of whoever created them black. The philosophy of Black Consciousness therefore expresses group pride and the determination of the black to rise and attain the envisaged self. Freedom is the ability to define oneself with one's possibilities held back not by the power of other people over one but only by one's relationship to God and to natural surroundings. On his own, therefore, the Black Man wishes to explore his surroundings and test his possibilities – in other words to make his freedom real by whatever means he deems fit. At the heart of this kind of thinking is the realisation by blacks that the most potent weapon in the hands of the oppressor is the mind of the oppressed. If one is free at heart, no man-made chains can bind one to servitude but if one's mind is so manipulated and controlled by the oppressor as to make the oppressed believe that he is a liability to the white man, then there will be nothing the oppressed can do to scare his powerful masters. Hence thinking along lines of Black Consciousness makes the black man see himself as a being complete in himself. It makes him less dependent and more free to express his manhood. At the end of it all he cannot tolerate attempts by anybody to dwarf the significance of his manhood.

In order that Black Consciousness can be used to advantage as a philosophy to apply to people in a position like ours, a number of points have to be observed. As people existing in a continuous struggle for truth, we have to examine and question old concepts, values and systems. Having found the right answers we shall then work for consciousness among all people to make it possible for us to proceed towards putting these answers into effect. In this process, we have to evolve our own schemes, forms and strategies to suit the need and situation, always keeping in mind our fundamental beliefs and values.

In all aspects of the black-white relationship, now and in
the past, we see a constant tendency by whites to depict blacks
as of an inferior status. Our culture, our history and indeed
all aspects of the black man's life have been battered nearly
out of shape in the great collision between the indigenous
values and the Anglo-Boer culture.

The first people to come and relate to blacks in a human
way in South Africa were the missionaries. They were in the
vanguard of the colonisation movement to 'civilise and educate'
the savages and introduce the Christian message to them. The
religion they brought was quite foreign to the black indigenous
people. African religion in its essence was not radically different from Christianity. We also believed in one God, we had
our own community of saints through whom we related to our
God, and we did not find it compatible with our way of life
to worship God in isolation from the various aspects of our lives.
Hence worship was not a specialised function that found expression once a week in a secluded building, but rather it
featured in our wars, our beer-drinking, our dances and our
customs in general. Whenever Africans drank they would
first relate to God by giving a portion of their beer away as a
token of thanks. When anything went wrong at home they
would offer sacrifice to God to appease him and atone for their
sins. There was no hell in our religion. We believed in the inherent goodness of man – hence we took it for granted that all
people at death joined the community of saints and therefore
merited our respect.

It was the missionaries who confused the people with their
new religion. They scared our people with stories of hell. They
painted their God as a demanding God who wanted worship
'or else'. People had to discard their clothes and their customs
in order to be accepted in this new religion. Knowing how
religious the African people were, the missionaries stepped up
their terror campaign on the emotions of the people with their
detailed accounts of eternal burning, tearing of hair and gnash-
ing of teeth. By some strange and twisted logic, they
argued that theirs was a scientific religion and ours a superstition – all this in spite of the biological discrepancy which is
at the base of their religion. This cold and cruel religion was
strange to the indigenous people and caused frequent strife

between the converted and the 'pagans', for the former, having imbibed the false values from white society, were taught to ridicule and despise those who defended the truth of their indigenous religion. With the ultimate acceptance of the western religion down went our cultural values!

While I do not wish to question the basic truth at the heart of the Christian message, there is a strong case for a re-examination of Christianity. It has proved a very adaptable religion which does not seek to supplement existing orders but – like any universal truth – to find application within a particular situation. More than anyone else, the missionaries knew that not all they did was essential to the spread of the message. But the basic intention went much further than merely spreading the word. Their arrogance and their monopoly on truth, beauty and moral judgment taught them to despise native customs and traditions and to seek to infuse their own new values into these societies.

Here then we have the case for Black Theology. While not wishing to discuss Black Theology at length, let it suffice to say that it seeks to relate God and Christ once more to the black man and his daily problems. It wants to describe Christ as a fighting god, not a passive god who allows a lie to rest unchallenged. It grapples with existential problems and does not claim to be a theology of absolutes. It seeks to bring back God to the black man and to the truth and reality of his situation. This is an important aspect of Black Consciousness, for quite a large proportion of black people in South Africa are Christians still swimming in a mire of confusion – the aftermath of the missionary approach. It is the duty therefore of all black priests and ministers of religion to save Christianity by adopting Black Theology's approach and thereby once more uniting the black man with his God.

A long look should also be taken at the educational system for blacks. The same tense situation was found as long ago as the arrival of the missionaries. Children were taught, under the pretext of hygiene, good manners and other such vague concepts, to despise their mode of upbringing at home and to question the values and customs of their society. The result was the expected one – children and parents saw life differently and the former lost respect for the latter. Now in African society it is a cardinal sin for a child to lose respect for his parent. Yet how can one prevent the loss of respect between child and parent when the child is taught by his know-all white tutors to disregard his family teachings? Who can resist losing respect for his tradition when in school his whole cultural background is summed up in one word – barbarism?

Thus we can immediately see the logic of placing the missionaries in the forefront of the colonisation process. A man who succeeds in making a group of people accept a foreign concept in which he is expert makes them perpetual students whose progress in the particular field can only be evaluated by him; the student must constantly turn to him for guidance and promotion. In being forced to accept the Anglo-Boer culture, the blacks have allowed themselves to be at the mercy of the white man and to have him as their eternal supervisor. Only he can tell us how good our performance is and instinctively each of us is at pains to please this powerful, all-knowing master. This is what Black Consciousness seeks to eradicate.

As one black writer says, colonialism is never satisfied with having the native in its grip but, by some strange logic, it must turn to his past and disfigure and distort it. Hence the history of the black man in this country is most disappointing to read. It is presented merely as a long succession of defeats. The Xhosas were thieves who went to war for stolen property; the Boers never provoked the Xhosas but merely went on 'punitive expeditions' to teach the thieves a lesson. Heroes like Makana* who were essentially revolutionaries are painted as superstitious trouble-makers who lied to the people about bullets turning into water. Great nation-builders like Shaka are cruel tyrants who frequently attacked smaller tribes for no reason but for some sadistic purpose. Not only is there no objectivity in the history taught us but there is frequently an appalling misrepresentation of facts that sicken even the uninformed student.

Thus a lot of attention has to be paid to our history if we as blacks want to aid each other in our coming into consciousness.

* Early nineteenth-century Xhosa prophet, sentenced to life imprisonment on Robben Island and drowned while escaping in a boat. Refusal by blacks to accept the truth of his death led to the mythical hope of his eventual return.

We have to rewrite our history and produce in it the heroes that formed the core of our resistance to the white invaders. More has to be revealed, and stress has to be laid on the successful nation-building attempts of men such as Shaka, Moshoeshoe and Hintsa.* These areas call for intense reserch to provide some sorely-needed missing links. We would be too naive to expect our conquerors to write unbiased histories about us but we have to destroy the myth that our history starts in 1652, the year Van Riebeeck landed at the Cape.

Our culture must be defined in concrete terms. We must relate the past to the present and demonstrate a historical evolution of the modern black man. There is a tendency to think of our culture as a static culture that was arrested in 1652 and has never developed since. The 'return to the bush' concept suggests that we have nothing to boast of except lions, sex and drink. We accept that when colonisation sets in it devours the indigenous culture and leaves behind a bastard culture that may thrive at the pace allowed it by the dominant culture. But we also have to realise that the basic tenets of our culture have largely succeeded in withstanding the process of bastardisation and that even at this moment we can still demonstrate that we appreciate a man for himself. Ours is a true man-centred society whose sacred tradition is that of sharing. We must reject, as we have been doing, the individualistic cold approach to life that is the cornerstone of the Anglo-Boer culture. We must seek to restore to the black man the great importance we used to give to human relations, the high regard for people and their property and for life in general; to reduce the triumph of technology over man and the materialistic element that is slowly creeping into our society.

These are essential features of our black culture to which we must cling. Black culture above all implies freedom on our part to innovate without recourse to white values. This innovation is part of the natural development of any culture. A culture is essentially the society's composite answer to the varied problems of life. We are experiencing new problems every day and whatever we do adds to the richness of our cultural heritage as long as it has man as its centre. The adoption of black theatre

* Famous tribal chieftains of, respectively, the Zulus, Basotho and Tswana.

and drama is one such important innovation which we need to encourage and to develop. We know that our love of music and rhythm has relevance even in this day.

Being part of an exploitative society in which we are often the direct objects of exploitation, we need to evolve a strategy towards our economic situation. We are aware that the blacks are still colonised even within the borders of South Africa. Their cheap labour has helped to make South Africa what it is today. Our money from the townships takes a one-way journey to white shops and white banks, and all we do in our lives is pay the white man either with labour or in coin. Capitalistic exploitative tendencies, coupled with the overt arrogance of white racism, have conspired against us. Thus in South Africa now it is very expensive to be poor. It is the poor people who stay furthest from town and therefore have to spend more money on transport to come and work for white people; it is the poor people who use uneconomic and inconvenient fuel like paraffin and coal because of the refusal of the white man to install electricity in black areas; it is the poor people who are governed by many ill-defined restrictive laws and therefore have to spend money on fines for 'technical' offences; it is the poor people who have no hospitals and are therefore exposed to exorbitant charges by private doctors; it is the poor people who use untarred roads, have to walk long distances, and therefore experience the greatest wear and tear on commodities like shoes; it is the poor people who have to pay for their children's books while whites get them free. It does not need to be said that it is the black people who are poor.

We therefore need to take another look at how best to use our economic power, little as it may seem to be. We must seriously examine the possibilities of establishing business co-operatives whose interests will be ploughed back into community development programmes. We should think along such lines as the 'buy black' campaign once suggested in Johannesburg and establish our own banks for the benefit of the community. Organisational development amongst blacks has only been low because we have allowed it to be. Now that we know we are on our own, it is an absolute duty for us to fulfil these needs.

The last step in Black Consciousness is to broaden the base of our operation. One of the basic tenets of Black Consciousness is totality of involvement. This means that all blacks must sit as one big unit, and no fragmentation and distraction from the mainstream of events be allowed. Hence we must resist the attempts by protagonists of the Bantustan theory to fragment our approach. We are oppressed not as individuals, not as Zulus, Xhosas, Vendas or Indians. We are oppressed because we are black. We must use that very concept to unite ourselves and to respond as a cohesive group. We must cling to each other with a tenacity that will shock the perpetrators of evil.

Our preparedness to take upon ourselves the cudgels of the struggle will see us through. We must remove from our vocabulary completely the concept of fear. Truth must ultimately triumph over evil, and the white man has always nourished his greed on this basic fear that shows itself in the black community. Special Branch agents will not turn the lie into truth, and one must ignore them. In a true bid for change we have to take off our coats, be prepared to lose our comfort and security, our jobs and positions of prestige, and our families, for just as it is true that 'leadership and security are basically incompatible', a struggle without casualties is no struggle. We must realise that prophetic cry of black students: 'Black man, you are on your own!'

Some will charge that we are racist but these people are using exactly the values we reject. We do not have the power to subjugate anyone. We are merely responding to provocation in the most realistic possible way. Racism does not only imply exclusion of one race by another – it always presupposes that the exclusion is for the purposes of subjugation. Blacks have had enough experience as objects of racism not to wish to turn the tables. While it may be relevant now to talk about black in relation to white, we must not make this our preoccupation, for it can be a negative exercise. As we proceed further towards the achievement of our goals let us talk more about ourselves and our struggle and less about whites.

We have set out on a quest for true humanity, and somewhere on the distant horizon we can see the glittering prize. Let us march forth with courage and determination, drawing strength from our common plight and our brotherhood. In time we shall be in a position to bestow upon South Africa the greatest gift possible – a more human face.

6

BLACK THEOLOGY AND
BLACK LIBERATION

by James H. Cone

Black Theology is relatively new to America. Although it has theological roots in the pre-Civil War black church, which recognised that racism and Christianity were opposites, the phrase 'Black Theology' is a phenomenon of the 1960s. One way of describing its appearance is to say that it is the religious counterpart of the more secular term 'Black Power', which means that it is a religious explication of the need for black people to define the scope and meaning of black existence in a white racist society. While Black Power focuses on the political, social and economic condition of black people, seeking to define concretely the meaning of black self-determination in a society that has placed definite limits on black humanity, Black Theology puts black identity in a theological context, showing that Black Power is not only *consistent* with the gospel of Jesus Christ, but that it *is* the gospel of Jesus Christ. My purpose is to investigate this thesis, analysing Black Theology in relation to black history, Black Power and the biblical message.

Black History

The black existential mood that expresses itself in Black Power and Black Theology stems from the recognition that black identity must be defined in terms of its African heritage rather than European enslavement. This was well expressed by James Baldwin:

> I was a kind of bastard of the West; when I followed my past, I did not find myself in Europe but in Africa. And this meant

that in some subtle way, in a really profound way, I brought to Shakespeare, Bach, Rembrandt, to the stones of Paris, to the Cathedral at Chartres and to the Empire State Building, a special attitude. These were really not my creations, they did not contain my history; I might search them in vain forever for any reflection of myself![1]

These words epitomise the spiritual and intellectual anguish that black people experience when they try to find meaning amid historical categories that are white and not black. They summarise the whole of black existence that is condemned to have its being in an environment inimical to black being. Black history has arisen to establish an authentic black past. Unlike European immigrants who came to America seeking escape from unjust tyranny, African presence was not by choice; we came as bondsmen, chained in ships. It was the slave-experience that shaped our memory of this land; and, perhaps, it should have been expected that the slave-event would not aid in our admiration of America, despite its rhetoric about 'equality' in 'the land of the free and the home of the brave'.

Unfortunately, our slavery was not limited to physical bondage. Added to physical domination was the mental enslavement of black people – the internalisation of the values of slave-masters. We were required to deny our African past and affirm those European values responsible for our enslavement. At worst, this meant accepting the slave-condition as ordained of God; and at best, it meant that Shakespeare and Bach set the standards of literary and musical creativity. In either case, our true African identity was denied. That was why Malcolm X. said: 'The worst crime the white man has committed has been to teach us to hate ourselves'. Black history changes all this.

It is clear now (as it has perhaps always been) that we are not Europeans, and thus George Washington, Thomas Jefferson and Abraham Lincoln are not our heroes. To accept them is to embrace Europe as the most significant cultural expression of our being. If culture is, as President Boumedienne of Algeria says, that which 'enables men to regulate their lives',[2] then Richard Nixon and Spiro Agnew cannot be the embodiment of our culture. Affirming them is tantamount to accepting our place as defined by slave-masters and denying the significance of Africa in the definition of black being. It is like trying to reconcile being and non-being, blackness and whiteness, and that is impossible. It is not possible to achieve a unified consciousness if we affirm two irreconcilable opposites. DuBois spoke of the agony of this experience:

> It is a peculiar sensation, this double-consciousness, this sense of always looking at one's self through the eyes of others, of measuring one's soul by the tape of a world that looks on in amused contempt and pity. One ever feels his two-ness – an American, a Negro; two souls, two thoughts, two unreconciled strivings; two warring ideals in one dark body, whose dogged strength alone keeps it from being torn asunder.[3]

The only cure for this double-consciousness is to move in the direction of the definition of blackness that is formed in the context of black liberation from white domination. Authentic black history is an investigation of the past through the eyes of black victims, a projection of our being into the unexplored depths of black consciousness – creating and affirming the *novum* of blackness in its undistorted African expression. In order to be free, we must be willing to move into uncharted dimensions of our being to create new value structures so that our understanding of blackness will not depend upon European misconceptions. It means realising that our history did not begin with the fifteenth-century European enslavement of Africans. Our origins go much further back into the pages of known and 'unknown' history. Known in the sense that we were there in the Egyptian Nile Valley, traditionally the cradle of civilisation: unknown in that the meaning of our personality is not dependent on the records of ancient history. The *present* reality of our encounter with blackness defines who we are. The new black consciousness arises from the need of black people to defend themselves against those who seek to destroy them. We know who we are in terms of doing what is necessary to protect ourselves and our families from the rats and filth, police departments and government officials. Our defence is at the same time a definition, a way of moving in the world, and it is programmed according to our need for liberation. The investigation of our past in the light of our liberation may be defined as Black Power taking on historical dimensions.

Black Power

To be exact, Black Power appeared in the spring of 1966, when Stokely Carmichael verbalised the unwillingness of black people to live under white definitions of their humanity. It may be true that the actual content of the phrase was not clearly defined, nor the dynamic of its implications in black-white relations clearly understood. Nevertheless this was the beginning of the will of black people to make public their utter distrust of white do-gooders and their displeasure with whites who try to tell them what their blackness ought to mean.

Black Power means that blacks are publicly declaring that whatever white people do, it will inevitably work against black freedom. Black people realise that they cannot change oppressors' attitudes by praying, singing gospel hymns, reading Scripture or preaching sermons. Neither can we change their view of the world simply by peaceably disobeying laws and allowing them to beat our women and children with police clubs. It just isn't true that if we try hard enough and wait patiently, the oppressors will eventually feel ashamed of their conduct and relinquish their power to enslave. Oppressors have no concern except to defend their own interests. We wait in vain for the Holy Spirit in this matter! Men in power will never admit that society rewards them far in excess of the service they render. The appeal to reason, religion, philosophy or sociology will not change their perspective. These disciplines are their tools and will inevitably serve as rationalisations of their own interests.

'There is nothing in common between a master and a slave', wrote Camus. 'It is impossible to speak and communicate with a person who has been reduced to servitude'.[4] This means partly that the presumption to power completely insensitises the master to the humanity of the slave, making him behave as if his own humanity depended on the enslavement of his brother. There is an 'infinite qualitative distinction' (to use a Kierkegaardian-Barthian phrase) between world views of master and slave; and if the slave intends to change his movement in existence, his first task is to inform the master what the limits are. The slave must be willing to define himself in terms of the silence of the master, realising that the latter's claptrap about life and happiness is a projection of his own ego, having nothing to do with authentic human existence. It is necessary to silence the master because the oppressor will never conclude that he should not be the ruler. The slave must not delude himself; freedom is not easy. 'Freedom', as Camus' Jean-Baptiste put it, 'is not a reward or a decoration that is celebrated with champagne. Nor yet a gift, a box of dainties designed to make you lick your chops. No, it's a chore . . . a long-distance race . . .'[5]

Black Power is the recognition that black freedom becomes a reality only when the victims of white racism declare that the oppressors have overstepped the bounds of human relations and that it is now incumbent upon black people to do what is necessary to bring a halt to the white encroachments on black dignity. The willingness to act on this conclusion means that blacks accept the risk of defining themselves. Like our forefathers who rebelled against slavery, we know that life is not worth living unless we are fighting against its limits.

Black Theology Defined

How are black history and Black Power related to Black Theology? Black history is recovering a past deliberately destroyed by slave-masters, an attempt to revive old survival symbols and create new ones. Black Power attempts to shape our present economic, social and political existence according to those actions that destroy the oppressor's hold on black flesh. Black Theology places our *past* and *present* actions toward black liberation in a theological context, seeking to destroy alien gods and create value-structures according to the God of black freedom.

The significance of Black Theology lies in the conviction that the content of the Christian gospel is liberation, so that any talk about God that fails to take seriously the righteousness of God as revealed in the liberation of the weak and downtrodden is not Christian language. Such talk may be 'religious' or 'churchly' and thus 'patriotic', but it has nothing to do with him who has called us into being and who came to us in Jesus Christ and is present with us today as Holy Spirit. To speak of the God of Christianity is to speak of him who has defined himself according to the liberation of the oppressed. Christian theology, then, pursuing its church-function, is the discipline that analyses the meaning of God's liberation in the light of Jesus Christ, showing that all actions that participate in the freedom of man are indeed the actions of God. Herein lies the heart of Black Theology's perspective of the theological task.

The definition of theology as an explication of the meaning of God's liberation of the oppressed arises essentially from two sources. The first is Biblical History.

According to the Bible, the God of Israel is known by what he is *doing* in history for the salvation of man. It is this critical dimension of divine activity that makes history and revelation inseparable in biblical religion. To see the revelation of God is to see the *action* of God in the historical affairs of men. God is not uninvolved in human history, as in the Greek philosophical tradition. The opposite is true: he is participating in human history, moving in the direction of man's salvation which is the goal of divine activity.

We must, of course, be cautious in our use of the word 'salvation', which means many things for different communities. For white oppressors it seems to have acquired a 'spiritual' connotation that is often identified with divine juice, squirted into the soul of believers, thereby making them better Christians and citizens. Understandably, salvation for them has little to do with the economic, political and social dimensions of human existence unless there are those who wish to challenge social injustice: men are then called upon to act out their salvation not only through silent prayer but by faithfully protecting the existing laws. An attack upon the state is tantamount to an affront to God, and all 'good' Christians must *show* their faith by protecting the sanctity of the nation. This view of the salvation of God is not only anti-biblical; it is dangerous, for it identifies God with oppressors, giving political and religious approval to the oppression of man.

The biblical view of salvation has an entirely different meaning. 'In the Old Testament salvation is expressed by a word which has the root meaning of 'to be wide' or 'to be spacious', 'to develop without hindrance' and thus ultimately 'to have victory in battle' (1 Sam. 14:45). To be saved meant that one's enemies had been conquered, and the saviour is he who has the power to gain victory.

He who needs salvation is one who has been threatened or oppressed, and his salvation consists in deliverance from danger and tyranny or rescue from imminent peril (1 Sam. 4: 3, 7: 8, 9: 16). To save another is to communicate to him one's own prevailing strength (Job 26: 2), to give him the power to maintain necessary strength.[6]

In the Old Testament, Yahweh is the Saviour *par excellence* because Israel's identity as a people was grounded in his liberating activity in the Exodus. 'You have seen what I did to the Egyptians, and how I bore you on eagles' wings and brought you to myself. Now therefore, if you will obey my voice and keep my covenant, you shall be my own possession among all peoples' (Exodus 19: 4–5). Through his election of this people God revealed that his righteousness is for the poor and weak, and that their salvation consists in his liberation of them from earthly bondage.

The same emphasis is found in the New Testament. Jesus is pictured as the oppressed one, who views his own person and work as an identification with the humiliated condition of the poor. The poor were at the heart of his mission: 'The last shall be first and the first last' (Matt. 20: 16). Thus he was always kind to traitors, adulterers and sinners, and the Samaritan came out on top in the parable. He said of the Pharisees (the religious oppressors of his day): 'Truly I say to you, the tax collectors [traitors] and harlots go into the kingdom – but not you' (Matt. 21: 31).[7] Jesus had little tolerance for the attitude of the middle- or upper-class religious snob which attempted to usurp the sovereignty of God and destroy the dignity of the poor. The kingdom is for the poor and not the rich because the poor has nothing to expect from this world while the entire existence of the rich is grounded in his commitment to wordly things. The weak and helpless may expect everything from God, while the oppressor may expect nothing because of his refusal to free himself from his own pride. It is not that poverty is a pre-condition for salvation, but according to our Lord, those who recognise their utter dependence on God and wait on his liberation despite the miserable absurdity of life are usually poor. Furthermore, it is not possible to be at the same time for Christ and also for the enslavement of men. For Christ salvation is not an eschatological longing for escape to a transcendent reality and neither is it an inward serenity which eases unbearable suffering. Rather it is God in Christ encountering man in the depths of his existence in oppression, and setting him free from all human evils, like racism, which hold him captive. The repentant man knows that though God's ultimate kingdom is in the future, yet Christ's resurrection means that even now God's salvation breaks through like a ray of 'blackness' upon the 'whiteness' of the condition of the oppressed, disclosing that oppressed man is not alone in the world. He who has called things into being is with the oppressed, and he will guarantee that man's liberation will become a reality of the land – and 'all flesh shall see it together'.

Our second source is Black Liberation. Paul Tillich says: 'Theology, as a function of the Christian church, must serve the needs of the church. A theological system is supposed to satisfy two basic needs: the statement of the truth of the Christian message and the interpretation of this truth for every new generation'.[8] If the truth of the Christian gospel is God's liberation that centres on the resurrection of Jesus Christ as the divine guarantee that he who is the Father, Son, and Holy Spirit has taken upon himself the oppressed condition of all peoples, then theology must ask: What is the significance of this message for our time? In what ways can we best show forth the meaning of God's liberating activity in the world so that the oppressed will be willing to risk all for earthly freedom? These questions are not easy, and they require a willingness to discard longstanding oppressive values and face the necessity to create new values according to the reality of divine liberation.

Taking seriously the necessity to make the Christian message of liberation relevant to our time, we conclude in America that Christian theology must be black. In a society where men are defined on the basis of colour for the purpose of humiliation, Christian theology takes on the colour of the victims, proclaiming that the condition of the poor is incongruous to him who has come to liberate us. Soulful James Brown was right when he said: Black is beautiful! It is beautiful because the white oppressors have made it ugly. Christians must glorify it because the oppressors despise it; we love it because they hate it. It is the Christian way of saying, 'To hell with your stinking white

society and its middle-class ideas about the world. It has nothing
to do with the liberating deeds of God'.

It is to be expected that white theologians, intrigued by their
own identification of whiteness with worth, will not endorse
Black Theology enthusiastically. Some will ignore it while
others will still respond: Theology is colourless! Such judgments
are typical of those who have not experienced the concreteness
of human suffering expressed through colour, or whose own
comfort has so long accepted a theology which is 'colourless'
only if by absence of colour one means 'white'.

The easy way out is to ignore Black Theology. It is analogous
to whites moving into suburbia because they cannot deal with
the reality of the black ghetto in the city. But what is more
interesting, though not surprising, is the white response that
theology does not come in colours. Those responsible for colour
being the vehicle of dehumanisation are now telling us that
theology is raceless and 'universal'. After nearly 400 years of
silence on this issue, this comes rather late. Black theologians
wonder why we did not hear the same word when people were
being enslaved in the name of God and democracy precisely
on the basis of colour. We also wonder where these 'colourless'
theologians were when people were being lynched because of
the colour of their skins. Something seems to be wrong with a
perspective that focuses only on the narrowness of the victims
of oppression. For everyone should know that whites and not
blacks are responsible for the demarcation of community on
the basis of colour. We blacks are merely the victims, and to
criticise the theology of the victims because it centres on that
aspect that best defines the limits of their existence seems to
miss the point.

Of course, Black Theology cannot waste its time trying to
demonstrate to oppressors the legitimacy of its work since it is
accountable only to its Lord, as he makes himself known through
the liberation of an oppressed community. It says: If Jesus
Christ is in fact the Liberator whose resurrection is the guarantee
that he is present with us today, then he too must be black,
taking upon his person and work the blackness of our existence,
and revealing to us what is necessary for our destruction of
whiteness. This means therefore that authentic theological
speech arises only from an oppressed community which realises

that its humanity is inseparable from its liberation from earthly bondage. All other speech is at best irrelevant and at worst blasphemous.

REFERENCES

1. *Notes of a Native Son*, Bantam 1968, p. 4.
2. Cited by Stanislas Adoteri, the *Black Scholar*, November 1969.
3. *The Souls of Black Folk*, Fawcett 1961, pp. 16–17.
4. *The Rebel*, Vintage 1946, p. 283.
5. *The Fall*, etc., Modern Library 1956, p. 132.
6. F. J. Taylor, *Theological Word Book of the Bible*, Macmillan 1960, under 'Save'.
7. For support of this translation see Günther Bornkamm, *Jesus of Nazareth*, Harper 1960, pp. 79, 203, and Joachim Jeremias, *The Parables of Jesus*, Scribners 1955, p. 100.
8. *Systematic Theology*, University of Chicago Press, p. 3.

7

WHAT IS BLACK CONSCIOUSNESS?

by Nyameko Pityana

Black people are notoriously religious, Religion permeates all
the depths of life so fully that it is not easy or even possible
sometimes to isolate it. It must be accepted then that a study
of Black Theology is a study of black consciousness or self-
awareness. In the context of the black community, the two
themes are intertwined. To the black people, religion is their
whole system of being. It is for this reason that the church (and
consequently a study of Black Theology) has added significance
to all those who are seeking avenues of self-expression and the
assertion of humanity and self-awareness. Thus the theme of
blackness is 'a quest for new values and definitions that are
meaningful and appropriate for black people and which give
substance and significance to their lives'.

The significance of this mood, this quest for new values, is
well summarised by Lerone Bennett, a black American historian:
'The overriding need of the moment is for us to think with our
own eyes. We cannot see now, because our eyes are clouded
by the concepts of white supremacy. We cannot think now,
because we have no intellectual instruments save those which
were designed expressly to keep us from seeing. It is necessary
for us to develop a new frame of reference which transcends
the limits of the white concepts, for white concepts have
succeeded in making black people feel that they are inferior;
they have wiped out their past history; or they have presented
it in such a way that they feel not pride, but shame. They
have successfully created the conditions that make it easy to
dominate a people. The initial step towards liberation is to
abandon the frame of reference to our oppressors, and create
new concepts which will release our reality.'

It has become imperative for us today to speak about Blackness and Consciousness because of the unfortunate history of events between black and white in South Africa. It is a history of continuous plunder of land and cattle by the European invaders, of devastation and the decimation of peoples, followed by their economic enslavement. It is a story of treacherous deeds, rapacity seasoned with sanctimonious hypocrisy, of 'treaties' that were not treaties but the cynical legalising of plunder, or the policy of 'divide and rule' carried out with systematic cunning to turn one group of black people against another.

It has been alleged with truth that the trader and the settler followed the missionary, who was the agent of European imperialism, working hand in hand with the colonial powers for the subjugation of the black people and the territorial extension of the imperialist power. The coming of Christianity set in motion a process of social change involving rapid disintegration of the tribal set-up and the framework of social norms and values by which people used to order their lives and their relationships. The measure of one's Christian conviction, the extent of one's love and charity was in preserving the outer signs and symbols of the European way of life – whether you had acquired European good manners, dressed as the European did, liked European hymns and tunes, etc. was all-important. The acceptance of the Christian church, the triumph of the missionary endeavour, meant the rejection of African customs. The tribal community was split widely asunder when Christianised blacks were encouraged to violate tribal customs. They were exempt from the morals and customs of the tribe which, in the light of Christian morality, were condemned as immoral. This meant the rejection of those values and rituals which held us together. European missionaries had attacked the primitive rites of the people, condemned our beautiful and soulful African tribal dances – the images of our gods – recoiling from their suggestion of sensuality. The black convert followed the same line, often with more zeal, for he had to prove how Christian he was through the rejection of his past and roots.

The coming about of Christianity brought with it a deep upheaval of African norms and values, a disintegration of families and tribes, and the cancerous money economy. The effect was to prepare blacks psychologically for the onslaught that was coming from the colonial rulers. They were dehumanised and had to accept their inferior status in the land of their birth. The early church in South Africa was never prepared to face up to the elements that stifled the national development and happiness of the black people. Black Consciousness has identified of the great myth designed to rob the black man of his soul and his human dignity, brought about by the white settlers with the able assistance of their handmaiden the Church, through blood and tears, in suppression and humiliation, through dishonest means, by force and subjugation of the sons of the soil. It is the liberating effect of this self-knowledge and awareness that we refer to as Black Consciousness.

I support Adam Small's definition of blackness: 'It is not colour of the skin in terms of which we see our blackness in the first place. It is, in the first place, a certain awareness, a certain insight.' He later on refers to this awareness as a phenomenon of pride and not inferiority. Ben Khoapa* supports this thesis when he says: 'The blackness we are talking about is not an emotional outburst – it speaks of a newly found self-love and self-affirmation.' No man can love another unless he loves himself; no group can value the truths maintained by others unless it perceives the essentials of its own truths. Khoapa further defines blackness in terms of 'developing a black perspective'. By this, he means 'searching for black identity, self-awareness and self-esteem and the rejection of white stereotypes and morals. It means stopping looking at things through white eyes and beginning to look at things through black eyes'.

These speakers come close to the S.A.S.O. definition of black consciousness. To us it is an attitude of the mind, a way of life. Consciousness goes a step further than mere awareness, for it seeks a positive and practical exhibition of one's awareness in deeds. It is a way of life – you must live and practise your consciousness in order to make it real. The S.A.S.O. policy manifesto goes on:

(i) the basic tenet of Black Consciousness is that the black man

* Black director of Sprocas II (second phase inaugurated early in 1972).

must reject all value systems that seek to make him a foreigner in the country of his birth and reduce his basic human dignity;

(ii) the black man must build up his own value system, and see himself as self-defined and not as defined by others;

(iii) the concept of Black Consciousness implies the awareness by the black people of the power they wield as a group, both economically and politically, and hence group cohesion and solidarity are important facets of Black Consciousness;

(iv) Black Consciousness will always be enhanced by the totality of involvement of the oppressed people, hence the message of Black Consciousness has to be spread to reach all sections of the black community.

Black Consciousness calls for a decultured being in the black society. It means 'a whole new vision, a totally different perspective, a penetration to the depths beneath the depth of blackness' (Lerone Bennett). Black Consciousness implies a vision of the heritage of our forefathers. It is the beginning of a new search for roots to anchor us firmly in the midst of a military struggle. It is not only a search for humanity but is an assertion and affirmation of the worth and dignity of the black man. Black Consciousness is indeed a hunger for solidarity with the oppressed people of this world. The real black people are those who embrace the positive description 'black' rather than the negatives of others who set themselves up as the standard, the criterion and hallmark of value. It is a positive confrontation with the self. Black Consciousness seeks for a social content of the lives of the black people, and to involve the one in the suffering of the others, for this has been the cornerstone of the traditional black community.

Having thus attempted to define and explain Black Consciousness, and to present the unfortunate activities of missionaries in the course of conquest, the stage is now set for a discussion of Black Theology. The need for a Black Theology must be seen in the context of the Church's role up to the present. The Churches are still an extension of the missionary ideal, being rooted in the white 'racist' system, and dominated by whites and the values of white superiority. The Church is white and it tells us that 'white Caesar can do no wrong'; instead of fighting against the real anti-Christ, it fights vigorously against

c*

those who are prepared to lose their lives that many might live. We have come to live with the contrasts between theory and practice – the white Church whose basic doctrine is love and equality between men is still an integral part of that social force, a white baasskap* on which is built the 'South African way of life', with it the consequent hatred between men, and effective subjugation of the black masses. Christianity is rooted in an exploitive, basically selfish cultural system.

Black Theology, then, is an extension of Black Consciousness. Theology is the study of God, but it also studies the relationship between man and man, and thus it must have an existential and social content. This will affect the ultimate good and shape the values of society. To black people the Church needs to be a haven where they can freely shed their tears, voice their aspirations and sorrows, present their spiritual needs, respond to the world in which they live and empty their souls out to God. Traditional belief provided psychological areas where uprooted men and women could find comfort, a sense of oneness and belonging together, and a recognition of being wanted and accepted. This is the true Church. But the Church, as at present constituted, is still foreign to the soul of the black man. He will not bring forth his love, fears, social relationships, thought-patterns, attitudes, philosophical dispositions, needs, aspirations, etc. The Church of the people must have its roots deeply established in the history and traditions of those who profess its doctrine. It is the black people themselves who must work out priorities in terms of their overriding aspirations, and their emotional and intellectual involvement in the struggles and sufferings of their people. They alone can do it.

If the Church is the greatest cause of the misshappen state of our country, the blackness of souls and culture alienation, it must in future work for the culture of liberation. It must go back to the roots of broken African civilisation, and examine the traditional African forms of worship, marriage, sacrifice, etc., and discover why these things were meaningful and whole-some to the traditional African community.

The awareness of this challenge motivated black students at the S.A.S.O. conference in July 1971 to pass a resolution

* Afrikaans, overlordship. As an official South African Government policy, gave way to apartheid under Dr Verwoerd.

affirming the belief that Black Theology 'is an authentic and positive articulation of the black Christians' reflection on God in the light of their experience'. It sees Christ as liberating men not only from internal bondage, but also from external enslavement. With James Cone we define Black Theology as 'a theology of liberation' that emancipates black people from white racism, and thus provides an authentic freedom for both black and white people. It affirms the humanity of white people in that it says 'no' to white oppression. It is an awareness by black people of the failure of the white establishment to work selflessly towards the values and ethics which Christianity claims to uphold. It is the will of the blacks to get their house in order and work towards the realisation of their aspirations, and their emancipation from the entanglements of an immoral society. This is where 'the twain' meet. Black Consciousness is also an awareness by a particular social group of people of its own situation in the world, and its expression of it by means of a concrete image. Both Black Theology and Black Consciousness are instruments of construction. Blackness gives a point of reference, an identity and a consciousness.

Black Theology seeks to commit black people to the risks of affirming the dignity of black personhood. 'We do this as men and as black Christians,' writes Cone. It calls upon all black people to affirm with Eldridge Cleaver: 'We shall have it on the Earth. The Earth will be levelled by our efforts to gain it.' In a nutshell, then, Black Theology concerns itself with liberation, and liberation presupposes a search for humanity and for existence as a God-created being.

The relationship between Black Theology and Black Consciousness is that one is a genus of the other. To be real in our situation, Black Theology must say something positive and meaningful to the black people. One such suggestion comes from James Ngugi: 'I believe the Church could return to (or learn lessons from) the primitive communism of the early Christian church of Peter and Paul, and the communalism of the traditional African society. With this, and working in alliance with the socialist aspirations of the African masses, we can build a new society to create a new man freed from greed, competitive hatred, and ready to realise his full potential in humble co-operation with other men in a just socialist society.'

CHRISTIANS
by James Matthews

Christians
that is what they term themselves
Sundays garbed in black and grey
they fill their churches' pews
faces turned towards the heavens
praising their god for their accorded task
rulers of the land; the chosen ones

Christians
their serfs seated in another church
told to serve without qualm
their master's demand

Christians
with pious right they sit and plot
dividing God's beaches and his land
ensuring that the fairest go to them
the little that is left
shared out among the many
who have no say and forced to
accept the desperation of their plight

Christians
unconcerned about those who sit and starve
whose crops, like themselves, die in arid soil
and others removed from the land they love

Christians
what welcome would they give God's son
confronted with the classification board
and identification card stating race
then consigned to his proper place
would he be banned for his message
that love has no colour connotation
that the brotherhood of man is all-embracing?

Christians
who deport priests for performing God's work
will not hesitate to proclaim an order
declaring the son of God an agitator.

8

CORPORATE PERSONALITY: ANCIENT ISRAEL AND AFRICA

by Bonganjalo Goba

(i) *Ancient Israel*

In attempting to assess the concept of the corporate personality in Israel, I do not intend to plunge you into the intricacies of Old Testament thinking, but to review briefly what this concept means and how it manifested itself in the life of the people of Israel. The term 'corporate personality' was first used by Wheeler Robinson in his attempt to understand the social consciousness of the people of Israel; the solidarity which existed and which seemed to govern their whole existence, which accompanied all forms of experience and understanding of history.

Corporate personality means the embodiment of the community in the individual. The individual represents the community to which he belongs. What the individual does affects the community, and vice versa. This concept of corporate personality is vividly illustrated in Israel, as Wheeler Robinson has observed, in the practice of blood revenge, which received religious sanction in the earlier part of the Old Testament. For example, David consulted the oracle of Yahweh concerning the cause of a protracted famine, and was informed that it was due to Saul's slaughter of the Gibeonites (2 Sam. 21: 1). We also find a portrayal of the concept in the story of Achan in Joshua 7: 24–26. In this story the concept of corporate personality also recognised that the whole nation was in the wrong through the act of one man. H. H. Rowley commented on this concept: 'The sociality and individuality of man in Israel were held together in the unity of a single view of the nature of man.' The group could be thought of as functioning through the individual member, who for the time being so completely represented it that he became identical with it. One discovers in this concept that life was 'felt' and the feelings and actions of an individual permeated the whole society to which he belonged. This was predominantly based on the feeling-relation, a feeling of 'sensed' and expressed belongingness. A man in this context was known in his context and history. He was not an isolated unit experienced as an isolated personality, but rather as a whole, for he derived his character from his involvement in the whole (both in history and environment), which stamped him with its specific character.

It is important for us to understand and to remember that this concept of corporate personality was not just simply environmental but was also historical, as I have mentioned previously. It is in this historical aspect that the cruciality of the ancestors in the Hebrew concept of corporate personality is discovered. In Israel the basic unit was the father's house – i.e. kinship. Unity stemmed from the strength of his personality, his ability to stamp his family with his character. This kinship determined one's actions and relations with the whole community. We shall discover how this idea of kinship in Africa is closely connected with the concept of corporate personality. In Israel the individual was required to act in accordance with the wishes and demands of his kinship. If he failed to do this, it affected the community to which he belonged. So one discovers in this concept of corporate personality, a unique relation of the individual to the community. The honour or dishonour of every member affects the entire group. There is a relational cohesion that overrides the wishes and feelings of the individual. A curse extends to the whole race and God visits the sins of the fathers on the children to the fourth generation (Ex. 20). A whole family is honoured if its head is brave, while the group is punished for a fault of its leader (2 Sam. 21). This solidarity is seen above all in the group's duty to protect its weak and oppressed members. This is what we also understand to be the obligation which lies behind the practice and institution of the *goel* (deliver). The significance of this conception is that Israel thus reveals, in a unique way, the solidarity which so many voiceless, oppressed people long for today.

(ii) Africa

Although we did not deal with the concept of time in relation to corporate personality in Israel, we will do this in our attempt to understand corporate personality in Africa. For an African time is an ontological phenomenon and pertains to existence or being. An African experiences time partly through the society which goes back many generations before his birth. Africans are not slaves to time; they create time.

It is important for us to understand this concept of time in Africa because it is bound up with the concept of corporate personality as it manifests itself in Africa. Human life in the context of African thought has another rhythm of nature which nothing can destroy. On the level of the individual one observes a rhythm which includes birth, puberty, initiation, marriage, procreation, entry into the community of the departed and finally entry into the company of the spirits. Life is regarded as a whole, and individuals live and are understood in this apprehension of life. The concept of corporate personality stems from this understanding of life; further it is evolved from a deep sense of kinship with all it implies, which as we know, is one of the strongest forces in traditional African life. Kinship, as John Mbiti* observes, is reckoned through blood and betrothal, engagement and marriage.

It is only from this context of kinship that we can possibly understand the concept of corporate personality in Africa. For as we know, it is kinship which controls social relationships between people in a given community, which governs marital customs and regulations, and which determines the very existence of an African and the behaviour of one individual towards another. Mbiti concludes: 'Indeed this sense of kinship binds together the entire life of the tribe.' It is in this context that we can speak of a corporate personality in Africa. What is significant is that behind the concept of kinship everybody is related to everybody else. This unique relationship extends vertically to include the departed and those yet to be born. This gives a sense of profundity, historical belongingness, deep-rootedness, or as Mbiti puts it, 'a sense of sacred obligation to extend the genealogical line'.

* Professor of Religious Studies, Makerere University, Uganda.

According to the kinship system, an individual does not and cannot exist alone. He owes his existence to other people including those of past generations and his contemporaries. He is completely part of the community, which creates and produces him. The individual depends on the corporate group. Only in terms of other people does the individual become conscious of his own being, his own duties, and his privileges and responsibilities towards himself and others. When an individual suffers he suffers not alone but with his kinsmen, his neighbours and his relatives whether dead or living. Whatever happens to the individual happens to the whole community to which he belongs, and whatever happens to the community happens to him as well. His life and that of the community is one and cannot be separated, for it transcends life and death. Hence he can say: 'I am because we are, and since we are, therefore I am.' This is the significant point in the understanding of the African view of man. A man's existence is a corporate existence.

We have a Zulu proverb, '*Zifa ngamvunye*', which means when one individual has done wrong the rest of the group to which he belongs is responsible. If a person steals a sheep, personal relations are at once involved, because the sheep belongs to a member of the corporate body – which illustrates another saying, '*Okwakho skwami*' (Sotho, meaning approximately 'what belongs to one belongs to all'), but how far the meaning of this expression goes must be left to the reader to decide. As such the offence and its consequences affect not only the thief but also the whole body of his relatives. The highest authority for the individual is the community of which he is a member.

As in Israel the concept of corporate personality manifests itself in everyday relationships, so also in Africa most of the communities are knit together by a web of kinship relations, and within these relationships every form of evil that a person suffers, whether it be a moral or a natural evil, is believed to be caused by members of his community. Similarly any moral offence that is committed is committed directly or indirectly against the members of his society.

What is the significance of this concept of corporate personality for us in South Africa today? When I say 'us', I am particularly referring to the black people – our struggle for liberation and to reaffirm our dignity. To discover our rightful place in this country, we need a deeply rooted sense of solidarity, a sense of a dynamic, relevant black community. For this we need to rediscover the meaning of this concept with all its practical implications; we need to look back at what we have lost and re-examine our present strategies. The Black Consciousness movement will be impoverished without this basic tenet of solidarity, of social consciousness, clearly expounded in the concept of corporate personality in Israel and particularly in African traditional thinking.

What we discover in the concept as it manifests itself in Israel and Africa is the unique idea of solidarity, a social consciousness that rejects and transcends individualism. Apart from this, one discovers a unique sense of a dynamic community, a caring concern that seeks to embrace all, a love that suffers selflessly for others. In this country many of us black people have allowed ourselves to be victims of individualism and capitalism. We are no longer living as a dynamic community; we have lost so much of our sense of corporate personality. Influenced by capitalism we have become materialistically self-centred, and the emphasis seems to be on individual enterprise and material acquisition for the individual – not for the black masses. Poverty is raging and swallowing many of our people, but the few among our black élite who have means are not bothered that thousands of blacks go to bed with empty stomachs. Many black children cannot go to school because they are hungry and poor. We have imbibed this individualism from the West, which is dividing and destroying our efforts to stand on our feet as a people able to help itself in a political and economic situation that is continuously dehumanising and oppressing us. I believe many of our black leaders who committed themselves to be agents of social change could have gone a long way, if they had inspired in the black masses this sense of corporate personality, or simply black solidarity. We have been fooled into believing the saying: 'Man is for himself and God for us all.' I would rather say everyman for all men and God for us all. The West today is discovering that the individualistic approach to life has brought many failures and difficulties, and is turning to the holistic approach to life as found in Africa. With this individualism has come domination, oppression and economic exploitation. Our political struggles have been weakened by our acquired individualism. Today, as black people in the country, we are divided and ruled, with no solidarity, no social consciousness, no common trust, no sense of common being. Black identity ought not to be seen simply in affirming our blackness, but in affirming our total black community.

Some may think it naive to attempt to rediscover our sense of corporateness as it was found in African traditional life, but I believe it to be absolutely necessary. Our situation and our liberation demand that we stand together and suffer together as a people. When one looks at the political and economic situation in this country, one discovers how this individualism which has crept into our black community has been exploited. A sense of mistrust and selfishness among ourselves is commonplace. If there is fear amongst us it is fear of black men. If it is murder in the streets of Soweto, it is murder committed by a black man. This situation has been created by the individualism that seeks to determine our politics, ethics and economics.

We saw, in our attempt to understand the concept of corporate personality, that the basic idea of kinship determined an individual's life and actions within a given community. The idea of everybody being related to everybody else created a dynamic communal life, and oriented an individual's responsibility towards the whole community. In our emphasis on personal autonomy and individual freedom, which has undermined the traditional authority of the community, weakened indigenous forms of social control and raised doubts about formerly accepted traditional norms, we have lost – or perhaps are losing – our kinship ties and thus our sense of corporateness. In our struggle to create a united black front, we must somehow remind ourselves of the significance of our living as a related people. Our blackness suffering disinheritance must be a force to make us a community with a united loyalty, purpose and commitment. In our situation in this unredeemed land the kinship ties that are needed must be those related to our blackness, a reclamation of our dignity, and above all those that transcend tribal loyalties. Our loyalty should be one committed to the liberation of the black community, and this can be achieved only when we stop living as if we were isolated individuals and begin to live corporately as children of one black family. When one of us suffers, or is persecuted, this must be the experience of us all. When one of us achieves success in his own enterprise or sphere of service, this must be our success too. Many of us, perhaps because of our education, have ceased to regard traditional norms as valid, but we must regard this norm of corporateness as overwhelmingly valid. We blacks in the South African situation can no longer live as isolated individuals. Our highest loyalty must be to our black community and this is what we seek in our need for black solidarity. This is the significance of the concept of corporate personality in South Africa today.

This unique dimension of corporateness is needed as one of our basic strategies in the Black Consciousness movement. If our aim is to bring about social and political change in South Africa, the inculcation of this concept in the minds of the people is necessary for the creation of a social cement – a united front. The black community must demand relevance, and this can be achieved if we take this concept seriously. We need a broad community coalition. The situation demands that all bodies, whether cultural, social or ecclesiastical, should come together – they must plan together, marshal their forces and pool their resources in order to uplift and liberate the black man. The meeting of various black organisations which took place at Edendale Ecumenical Centre, Pietermaritzburg,* was an attempt to embark on this task of creating a united black front. Our effectiveness in our Black Consciousness movement will depend on our willingness and determination to act and stand corporately on all issues that affect us as black people.

Today the slogan of self-help is heard far and wide. Many black African governments and social organisations are geared towards the principle of self-help and self-determination. Our role in attaining black solidarity demands that we adopt this principle ourselves. We can no longer subject ourselves politically and economically to the paternalism of the white people. For a long time we have been looking to the white world for our material survival. We cannot accept this any longer because the material wealth and resources of South Africa belong to us

* Cf. p. vii.

and are a direct result of our efforts. A crucial basis of our struggle for self-determination should be our corporateness, our sense of social consciousness. We can help ourselves if we trust ourselves. As black people with very limited resources, we need to marshal our forces and be determined to help ourselves to do our own thing in education, community development and church life. We can achieve tremendous success if we are a solid dynamic black community. It should be our aim to get rid of the mentality prevalent amongst our black masses of white dependence. This is part of our venture to express our dignity, our ability to be men, and our human responsibility to our fellow-men and our country. The significance of this concept of corporate personality is that we should, as leaders, ministers and individuals, be responsible to our community, which means that we must now do things for ourselves as black people rather than allow certain people to do things for us. Again this means that we must take the initiative in all activities and projects which affect our people. It is in helping ourselves as a black people that our social consciousness will grow and blossom. In our corporateness we will all be involved in helping one another and our people, in the poverty-stricken areas, in the urban ghettos of Soweto and in the resettlement areas. Again, if we seek to live corporately, we will not accept the sight of thousands of our own black people illiterate and thousands of our black children deprived of education. Self-determination is a challenge to the black community to share its resources. We can no longer allow poverty to thrive amongst our people, but we are called upon to share our money and our food, and this can only come when every one of us becomes responsible to our black community.

Time does not allow us to complain about what we have lost or to resort to self-pity. It demands that we do something for ourselves. This means that businessmen can no longer say 'This is my shop' or 'This is my garage'. It is 'for the people'. Individuals too can no longer act or think in terms of their own particular interest but for the community. What the individual achieves in commerce, education and politics will be the achievement of the community as a whole.

Today the key word for change is 'involvement'. If we accept the need for a corporate personality in our situation in South

Africa our involvement in what is happening in our midst becomes necessary. We can only be socially conscious if we are involved in the life of the people. Again we can only be concerned for one another if we are involved. So many of us are remote from the everyday experiences of our black people. There is a gap between the black élite and the ordinary black man. We have allowed our acquired intellectualism to separate us from the ordinary people. Today when we speak of the Black Consciousness movement, we immediately think of students in S.A.S.O. and a few clerics. The rest of the people are not involved. If black solidarity is to achieve anything this gap cannot be allowed to exist. This means that each one of us should be involved in the lives of our fellow-men. We must be able to share our views and communicate with the ordinary black person in the street. Black intellectualism must not become a monopoly of the few but must involve itself practically in the issues that affect us all in South Africa today. Involvement in this context means taking seriously the dignity of every black person in spite of intellectual differences and working for the maintenance and growth of the dignity of every black person. This is the significance of the concept of corporate personality for us in this country today.

Finally, God is calling every black person to sacrifice his or her individual longing and luxury to long for a dynamic community of love where every black person finds meaningful existence breaking through oppression, injustice and disinheritance. The relevance of Christ, the Man of Nazareth, who vividly exemplified the corporate personality of Israel, is that *in Him* our blackness is redeemed. His message of love – for our neighbour as for ourselves – is crucial for us. If we aim to live and act corporately as black people, then every black person is called to love every other black person as he loves himself. We are called to be a sharing coherent community, and it is in being this community that we shall go forward gallantly to meet the forces that dehumanise and oppress us. Black Solidarity is the answer, provided a black corporate personality exists.

9

BLACK THEOLOGY:
A PERSONAL VIEW

by Mokgethi Motlhabi

The emergence of Black Theology with its doctrine of the 'total' liberation of the black man has become one of the most controversial subjects affecting him in present-day South Africa. This has been the case since the call made in 1969 by the five Catholic priests for the Africanisation of the Church in our country and the recognition of the black clergy; and since the proclamation by the South African Students' Organisation of the need for a Black Consciousness and Black Identity. This Black Liberation move and the means towards its achievement are seen from the same perspective by both the 'Black Theologian' and the black student.

The distinction which makes Black Consciousness a 'secular' movement and Black Theology a 'religious' movement I find unfortunate. Perhaps the sole purpose of this distinction is to indicate a point of view, so that while the object for both movements is fundamentally the same, the theologian's approach towards its realisation is slightly different from that of the philosopher, the social scientist or the politician. Nonetheless the distinction gives the impression of still maintaining a dualistic view of the world, according to which the world is divided into spiritual and material, the former being sacred and the latter profane. To the profane world belongs secular society and to the sacred the Church, as the higher caste. The Church is regarded as being in the world but not belonging to it. Thus it seeks the conversion of the world, not in the sense of helping it to strive for perfection within itself, but of denying itself (as if regretting its being), or abstracting and projecting itself towards some kind of ideal perfection which always remains for it an eschatological mystery. A kind of envy is to be expected on the part of the world which does nothing to help it towards self-fulfilment but only hastens its self-destruction. Emphasis on this kind of perfection, divorced from day-to-day experience and doing nothing to improve the life situation (which is what needs perfection), obstructs the effectiveness of the Church's mission and retards or utterly obscures the understanding of the Scriptures.

One of the essential characteristics of our world is that it is in the process of becoming, and 'becoming' is a dynamism towards the realisation of 'being', which is its perfection. Thus perfection is 'happening' to the world; it is not extraneous to it. 'Becoming', in this way, presupposes 'being', so that at each stage of its becoming the world *is*, but *is not*; it *is perfect* but *is not perfect*. It is thus always in the process of becoming itself: it *happens* to itself. In this process the world continually becomes *other than itself within itself*: it finds a certain fulfilment. It is clear, therefore, that perfection for the world does not mean its being extracted from its earthly situation into some abstract 'Christlike' one. It means that Christ is happening to it in its authentic, existential situation. Socially this means happening to oneself through one's environment and through other selves, and a mutual assistance of selves within society towards the happening of each individual within society and the happening of society as a whole.

It means Christ happening to man in his daily experience and his daily communication with his fellow-men. Communication, however it occurs, is an indication of Christ's presence and his working among men, whether we recognise him or not. Striving for communication with other men is thus automatically striving for Christ. Hence Christ is the very perfection of man. He is the kind of being we are directly striving for in our Christian or any religious faith (we often speak of anonymous Christians); further, he is the being we are indirectly striving for in our other human communications. So communication among men implies a search for Christ prompted by himself; and hope in the perfection of this communication in Christ, when all men will realise their oneness in him, and their authenticity as the mystical body of Christ. We have found it expedient to speak of a Black Theology as a liberation theology because of the constitution of man and his nature as a communicative being. Man's present constitution is such that he is, according to Luther, in the state of 'fallenness', where his 'original state' of communication has been affected. In his obsession with the idea of freedom and independence, as created in God's image, man became so snatching that he soon found God to be an obstacle on his way towards 'complete' freedom. That is to say, being only the image of God, man's freedom was only a reflection of God's freedom, and not freedom itself, for only God is freedom by definition. He knew that as long as he recognised God he would remain in a subordinate position. On the other hand, he could not 'unseat' God, for God is his very being: there can be no image without that of which it is the image. The only alternative was to expel God from his mind, and *pretend* that God did not exist. In this way he 'became' master of himself and master of his environment.

Thus it is that man alienated himself from God. But since God is the uniting element between man and man, alienation from God meant alienation from his fellow-men and consequently alienation from himself. This means a state of confusion, so that man continuously lives a lie in the name of truth: and he knows it. Now this was from the beginning a deliberate act on the part of man, and if it continues, it is still deliberate. If this act of alienation continues to harass other men morally, it is a crime, and since it is also directed against God, through those who are its victims, it is a sin, which is nothing but a deliberate act of alienating man from himself, his fellow-man and his God. Our situation in South Africa is such that we need a personal, psychological liberation from ourselves and what enslaves us; a social, political and economic liberation in relation to our fellow-men, the more so across the 'colour bar'; and a religious liberation in relation to God. Each of these cases implies communication. This, when understood from the black man's point of view in his situation, and the means the black man employs towards its realisation, is called Black Consciousness. Black Theology is its theological aspect.

The task of fostering this communication has been entrusted to every man by virtue of his nature as a social and communicative being. In Christian tradition it is regarded as having been entrusted to the Church 'pastorally', as a community. Therefore the Church has a direct mission towards the fostering of a 'human community', which should necessarily imply Christ's presence. Christianity must permeate – i.e. carry Christ – through every sphere of human life. So Christianity begins in the fact of daily man-to-man communication, which gradually leads man nearer to Christ. It should not be an abstraction, but a daily experience in which we find Christ in our fellow-men. The closer we are to our fellows, the closer we are to Christ. Christianity, therefore, means Christ's presence in the world among men sacramentalised in our fellow-men.

For this reason, as stated at the beginning, I find the kinds of distinction implied in the treatment of the 'two worlds' no longer tenable; but it may possibly serve as a means of accommodating a protagonist who might be prejudiced against a seemingly alien title: either Black Consciousness or Black Theology.

Having thus examined the phenomena from which man needs to be liberated, we are now able to go deeper into the meaning of Black Theology. It is that aspect of Black Consciousness which seeks to relate God and the gamut of religious values to the black man in his situation in South Africa. To be black in our country means first, to be the victim of apartheid and the object of colonisation, disinheritance and exploitation. It also means, in religious circles, to be pagan, barbaric and almost damned; and all because of the colour of one's skin, which is not white. In Black Theology the term 'black' only secondarily connotes colour, which popular white parlance in South Africa prefers to call 'non-white'. It denotes all the oppressed people in our country irrespective of colour (which cannot be white, of course), nationality or creed. It thus embraces all the African people, the Indians and the so-called Coloureds. Black Theology, therefore, seeks to relate God as both man's creator and his liberator to all these people in their entire situation, not only religious but also social, political and economic. God's word and sustenance permeates the whole of man's life and being by virtue of his very creation in God's image.

Although Black Theology is a theology of liberation, it is contrasted to the traditional 'salvation of the soul' theology in

that it does away with all dualistic overtones which divide
man from himself and concentrate on one part only. In Black
Theology man is regarded as a complete whole, a mind-body-
soul composite in, and confronted by, a complete situation.
By liberating the black man psychologically, Black Theology
makes the black man ready to look around himself and see
what it is that ails him precisely as himself, as black. It calls
for a consciousness, for it recognises that it is because a man is
black that he is oppressed.

Black Theology is not a new theology nor is it a proclamation
of a new gospel. It is merely a revaluation of the gospel message,
a making relevant of this message according to the situation of
the people. It is a re-interpretation of the Scriptures in the light
of the existential situation of our daily black experience. Its
advocates believe that Christ not only has something to do
with and something to offer to *my soul*, but to *me* in my entirety
and my condition here and now, according to what we read
in Luke 4: 18: 'The Spirit of the Lord has been given to me,
for he has anointed me. He has sent me to bring the good news
to the poor, to proclaim liberty to captives and to the blind
new sight, to set the downtrodden free, to proclaim the Lord's
year of favour'. Christ is, therefore, taken almost literally when
he says 'Now he is God, not of the dead, but of the living; for
in him all men are in fact alive' (Luke 20: 38).

It is necessary here to clarify some of the misunderstandings
which bring many people into opposition to Black Theology.
These base themselves unwittingly on the word 'black', contend-
ing that theology is only one and has no colour. This is a trap
that one falls into when not prepared to listen to another's
views but, being already biased, waits only to catch you out
with a word that might seem wrongly used, in spite of its given
definition in the case. I have already said what 'black' is taken
to mean in Black Theology. Its true meaning is co-extensive
with suffering, and since the suffering lot of the majority in
South Africa is 'not white', 'black' is rightly used, affirming that
whiteness is not the only value in relation to which everything
else should be considered. Black Theology is thus theology from
the viewpoint of the suffering, just as Barth writes from a
Lutheran and German viewpoint or Schillebeeckx from a
Roman Catholic and Dutch viewpoint. So if the real meaning

of 'black' in this case is suffering, then why not call a spade a spade? But what is important is not the name so much as its import; hence the definition of Black Theology as the theology of liberation from suffering.

A further objection is that Black Theology is racist and un-Christian since it does not seem to have any regard for the white people in South Africa. It is therefore said to be a successful piece of indoctrination by the South African policy of separate development. But these are the very bonds from which Black Theology seeks to liberate the black man, the very bonds that are seen to preoccupy his mind to the extent that he can no longer even meditate on his God or find the opportunity to offer sacrifice unhindered. When a man's mind is prevented from thinking on his god, God dies because he no longer manifests himself in the life of this man as its sole author, and so as its sole director. But as a man's mind is by nature God-oriented and God-inspired, and as his entire life and being is inconceivable without God, the death of God means for him the birth of idols. Now these may be a fabrication of man himself or they may be what those who rule his mind present to him as 'God'. Where a religion is concerned this may be the result of a wrong kind of interpretation, springing from a different background and outlook from that of the people to whom it wishes to present God.

Unfortunately, this seems to have been, and still remains, the case in the presentation of the Christian message to the black people in our country. No doubt, most of the gospel message still remains a foreign gospel to the indigenous people. Granted that Christianity was well adapted to Western culture and values, very little has been done to adapt and relate the Christian tenets to the African way of life and culture. Christianity was from the beginning brought to the black man wrapped in Western culture and Western values, and no distinction was drawn between the two (Christianity and Western culture). Thus any black man wishing to become Christian had to embrace the whole of the Western values without due analysis and understanding, and had to renounce his entire background as paganism and superstition. An idol was presented in place of God, so that the black man still needs to be liberated from idolatry. Thus for the black man the death of God and the birth of idols is seen as a theological perversion: the mis-direction, misinterpretation and mispresentation of God and his gospel to the black people in this country. No doubt this was done by some with the best of intentions and goodwill. But contributing to this already messed-up gospel was the stand the hierarchy adopted in identifying itself with the State in its evil policies. Today the hierarchy proclaims by word of mouth what it seldom, if ever, practises. Most often its practices, even within the church structures, are contrary to the true gospel and to what the Church says in Biblical exposition, if it says any-thing at all. It is clear that, once confidence in it has been lost, the Church can no longer speak convincingly about what it stands for. What remains is an examination of conscience and the realisation of the need for change. This is what Black Theology seeks to do.

Black Theology bears the concern of every Christian for the spread of the gospel, the reorientation and rehabilitation of the people of God. It is therefore not denominational, in the sense of being advocated by a particular church or creed, nor does it advocate a schism from traditional churches. It is only concerned with adopting the most, and perhaps the only, realistic way of spreading the gospel for the benefit of the individual and society, realising the uniqueness of every situa-tion. Thus the Transvaal Regional Seminar on Black Theology (held at Hammanskraal, 1971) resolved that it is 'not a theology of absolutes, but grapples with the existential situation. Black Theology is not a theology of theory, but a theology of action and development. It is not a reaction against anything – except irrelevancy – but is an authentic and positive articulation of our reflection on God in the light of our black experiences.'

The resolution concludes: 'As a consequence we turn our backs on the biased interpretation of the Christian message which the white-dominated churches have been feeding to the black people. We understand Christ's liberation to be a libera-tion not only from circumstances of external bondage but also a liberation from circumstances of internal enslavement.'

I O

AN AFRICAN EXPRESSION
OF CHRISTIANTIY

by Akin J. Omoyajowo

When G. C. Oosthuizen gave the title of *Post-Christianity in Africa* to a recent publication the impression was that he seemed unable to appreciate the problem of the Church in Africa. However, this same author went on to admit that the main problem of the Church in Africa is the Church herself, because 'in so many ways it is unrelated to Africa'.[1]

It is common among many Africans nowadays to describe the Christian religion as an imported religion – the religion of the colonial masters – and to feel that it should be replaced by indigenous religion. We only need to be reminded that by the fourth century Christianity had been firmly established in North Africa, and that African church leaders like Tertullian, Cyprian and Augustine made substantial contributions to the shaping of Christian theology. But this strong North African Church did not survive the Arab invasion in the seventh century. The Church was easily swept away. This was due mainly to the fact that 'it was not truly an African Church; its members were from the Roman and Greek middle classes, the colonists who lived apart from the indigenous peoples'.[2] The indigenous population of Berbers was only nominally christianised.

At an earlier period, the first attempt at establishing a purely African Church had failed with the crushing of the Donatist Movement. 'By crushing Donatism with the aid of the Emperor', Professors J. F. A. Ajayi and E. A. Ayandele have observed, 'The Roman Catholic Church killed a truly African Church and with it the social, cultural, and political aspirations and identity of the Berbers'.[3] Although Professor Thompson of the Department of Classics, University of Ibadan, does not quite accept the social, economic and political implications of the controversy, he agrees that within a few years 'the dispute had split the African Church into two hostile factions: Donatists and Catholics, the latter remaining true to the established Catholic Church'.[4] It is significant that the Emperors had become exasperated because of the futility of all their efforts to crush the schism when St Augustine, incidentally a fellow-African, brilliantly succeeded in nailing up the coffin of the movement. Whatever the motivating factors, the fact remained that the Donatists were concerned to establish an exclusively African Church, which to them was the only pure, true and holy Church – the Church of the martyrs.

Perhaps this was the idea behind the attitude of the Monophysites in Egypt who rejected the decisions of the Council of Chalcedon in 451, backed out of the Catholic Church and constituted themselves into the Coptic Church opposed to Byzàntine Orthodoxy. One cannot ignore the fact that in spite of the fate of the early North African Church, the Coptic Church has survived there, refusing to die in the face of sustained hostility from the Muslims for centuries.[5]

In the second phase of Christianity in Africa from the fifteenth to the eighteenth centuries, very little was achieved especially in its centre in the Congo, and the little could not be sustained for long. In the Cape Province where Christianity gained some footing, 'it became the monopoly of the incorrigibly opionated, ultra-selfish and Bible-reading Afrikaner frontiersmen, who had begun to view themselves alone as the legitimate owners of the world of South Africa and confirmed, predestined inheritors of Heaven'.[6]

Africans at this time could not see Christianity as their religion especially as its 'Apostles' were easily seen as the prosecutors of the trans-Atlantic slave-trade. There was also what Professor Ayandele has described as the naked barbarism of the Portuguese settlers at Sao Thome and in San Salvador which 'neutralised the efforts of missionaries in the Congo Basin.'[7] Africans had not the opportunity to study the religion and to see it from their own perspective.

It was during the third phase which began in the nineteenth

century and which is still with us, that Christianity succeeded in reaching the widest areas of the continent of Africa especially South of the Sahara. The phenomenon of African active participation in the spread of the religion in Africa enabled Africans to recognise its relevance to their way of life, and with this the desire to employ the most effective methods to drive home its message to fellow-Africans.

But also in this phase we can recognise other stages of development. There were the early African missionaries who, according to Professor Idowu,[8] were educated by methods and along the lines known to their educators and whose Christianity 'was heavily tinged with Western culture'. Even Samuel Ajayi Crowther, the first African to be consecrated bishop in the Anglican Church, 'was only nominally a native bishop; in practice essentially a missionary and in fact the symbol of a race on trial'.[9] Crowther used the mission house as the nucleus of civilization and the centre of a new way of life.[10] He once told a conference of Onitsha rulers and missionaries that he could not agree that converts should join in the customary rites, which was one reason why the mission villages were physically separated from the towns. Crowther clearly rejected many traditional practices, and refused to baptise polygamists. Of course, the mere fact that Africans were being accorded positions of leadership in the Church was becoming offensive to white missionaries, a point of view championed by Henry Townsend, who protested vigorously against the choice of Crowther as bishop. He contended that 'if they [Africans] hear that a black man is our master, they will question our respectability,'[11] and told Henry Venn, the C.M.S.* Secretary, that no African was fit to be a leader 'at the present time', whatever the opinion he could form or the statement he could make or the advice he could give.[12]

We see something of his frustration in his letters. 'It is reported here that we are to have a black bishop, a bishop Crowther,' he wrote in January 1864, 'a bishop of the Niger to reside at Lagos and to have nothing to do with us. . . . I believe it will be done if the C.M.S. can do it, but it will be a let-down.'[13] Even after the consecration of Bishop Crowther, the old missionary did not let sleeping dogs lie. He wrote to

* Church Missionary Society.

Venn in November 1864: 'It is now expected that we should voluntarily place ourselves under the superintendence of Bishop Crowther. If white men had been accustomed to look up to one as Superintendent, it would have been easy to change one for another'. And then he insisted: 'I do not believe in his [Crowther's] power to become head of the Church here, notwithstanding. He is too much of a native.'[14]

Thus, it was not difficult for the white missionaries to discredit Bishop Crowther and his African clergy, especially as colonial rule set in, bringing a dramatic swing to an almost absolute missionary control of the Church by the end of the nineteenth century.

This precipitated in West Africa the agitation for the promotion of the indigenous culture, by James Johnson from within and Edward Blyden from without. The turning-point was finally reached at the turn of the century when the African churches came into existence in protest against the unsympathetic condemnation of polygamy by white missionaries and against white domination of the Church hierarchy. This was the second stage. It is necessary to point out, however, that the African churches did not really go further than the establishment of an African leadership of the Church. Their liturgy and other practices remained essentially alien.

Even though James Johnson's dream of the establishment of a purely indigenous African Church did not materialise (and in fact the leaders of the African Churches were disappointed because he failed to secede with them), the plain truth was that the time was not too far away when this would become a reality. It had to wait for the emergence of the independent African Church movements. The independent Church movements now number highest in South Africa. While in 1913 there were only 30, 800 had emerged by 1948, and by 1960 there were 2,200:[15] in East Africa there were over 200 by 1967.[16] It is said that there were no fewer than 6,000 of these movements in the whole of Africa.

Reasons for their formation are various. T. A. Beetham has suggested a few: 'A revolt against European domination in Church or State (the latter being the case in Southern and East Africa); a revolt against the practice of the Churches in regard to polygamy (as was the case with the African Churches);

a revolt against limitations of spontaneous expression in worship, such as drumming, handclapping and dancing, or in the application of the Christian faith to healing and the related world of witchcraft.'[17] Happily Beetham quickly added that revolt was not the only factor; but that 'the response of the Holy Spirit to the questing spirit of man, in a situation where the existing Churches were not helping him to meet his deepest need, was to inspire this man or that woman with the gift of prophecy.'[18]

This brings us to what we must now recognise as an African expression of Christianity. In their zeal to save the souls of Africans from eternal damnation, the early missionaries mixed Christian principles with Western culture, not to say beliefs. Christianity became identical with Westernism. As Professor Idowu aptly pointed out,[19] 'the Church in Africa came into being with prefabricated theologies and traditions'. The situation was further confused by the sectarian characteristics of the foreign missionary bodies, each with its own distinctive tradition. The god that was introduced to Africa was a completely foreign god, and this robbed Christianity of its universality. In spite of its civilising and educating nature, this religion became spiritually unsatisfactory. The African could not see its relevance to his life, and the result was an ambivalent spiritual life. In times of crisis, the believer would revert to traditional measures. The need for a spiritual revolution became urgent, and it soon became manifest that the Holy Spirit could speak directly to the African to save the Church in Africa from the extinction that had been the fate of the North African Church centuries before. The Holy Spirit descended and called out Africans to express Christianity in language that would be understandable and meaningful to the people. Thus came into existence the phenomenon of the African Independent Churches.

In treating this question I shall limit my illustrations to West Africa where the movements were not racially or politically inspired as were similar movements in Southern and East Africa. They are known in Nigeria mainly as Aladura movements, and in Ghana Professor Baeta calls them Prophet movements.[20] As Professors Ajayi and Ayandele observed,[21] the movements 'sought to establish the Christianity of the Bible as they saw it, devoid of its European accretions and in harmony with Africa's cultural heritage'. Theirs was an attempt to evolve their own forms of liturgy, hymnology, etc., such as would make the Africans feel at home as they worship Jehovah in spirit and in truth.[22]

They represented a reaction against the European complexion of the Western-oriented Churches with their completely pre-fabricated theology and Christianity from their own perspective and to worship as Christian Africans. Here was a desire to introduce into Christianity what Idowu[23] describes as the 'emotional depth' which is an integral part of the spiritual make-up of the African but which is almost non-existent in the Western-oriented Churches.

Forerunners of these movements were the travelling evangelist William Wade Harris, the Grebo from Liberia who, travelling through the Southern Ivory Coast in 1914, brought more men and women to the Christian faith than any missionary or evangelist has yet done in West African history, and Garrick Sokari Braide of the Niger Delta who in a space of two years during the First World War won more converts to Christianity than the C.M.S. has won in the same area in the previous fifty years.[24]

The Independent Indigenous Churches in West Africa are a twentieth-century phenomenon, and whatever other factors aided their emergence, we must see them as essentially religious movements which have at least provided the much longed for spiritual home for African Christians.

In view of the fundamental and basic areas of agreement among these movements, it is reasonable to discuss the features which they all share in common and which accord them the right to be recognised as the African's approach to Christianity. (There are several of them – the Faith Tabernacle 1923, the Cherubim and Seraphim 1925, the Church of the Lord Aladura 1930, the Apostolic Group of Churches 1930s, etc., etc., all originating in Nigeria.) These movements were the results of the spiritual experiences of their founders – usually divine revelations in dreams, trances or visions. Whatever the form of the revelation, they usually came in answer to the founders' dissatisfaction with the spiritual situation in the Church. As Ajayi and Ayandele pointed out, these founders were 'people yearning for spiritual satisfaction, seeking and obtaining answers to questions for which there are no solutions in the Western-established Churches. In the Aladura Churches, they find psychological and emotional security. They live in a world of prayerfulness where after the rough and tumble of daily life, they could get far away from the maddening crowd. . . . Within the Aladura Churches, the African emerges, as he has always been in the traditional setting, a very religious person'.[25]

Now to the crucial question: how are these Churches and movements an African expression of Christianity? Why are they regarded as Christian at all and not just a radically refined form of traditional religion blended with elements that are basically Christian?[26]

First, as to doctrine. The indigenous Churches generally accept the basic doctrines of the Church: they believe strongly in the Bible, regarding it as the sole authority for the Christian. Their approach is somewhat fundamentalist, hence their incessant quotations from the Bible. There have been members of these Churches who could quote accurately from practically all the books of the Bible. Their theology, therefore, is essentially Biblical theology. They also believe in the Holy Trinity, in God the Father, God the Son and God the Holy Ghost, and ask no questions about the mysteries of the godhead or the union of the divine and the human in Jesus Christ. They are not interested in debates about the Jesusness of Christ or the Christness of Jesus. After all, such inexplicable mysteries are not lacking in the traditional beliefs.

They also recognise the radical and political neutrality of Christianity which is why they believe that God could send them out on special missions despite their unletteredness and lack of social sophistication. They believe in the dispensation of the Holy Spirit and recognise the spiritual sterility of the Western-related Churches. They refuse to rationalise, as this will be tantamount to sacrilege. Theirs has always been a simple faith in God and an unalloyed confidence that God will surely and faithfully fulfil what He has promised to believers in Jesus Christ. It is significant that the Aladura Churches generally do not deny any of the verities of the Christian faith. They were out not to corrupt the faith, but to make it speak to Africans in a language comprehensible to them.

Secondly, liturgy. Here the Indigenous Churches have gained

full marks. Idowu has rightly defined liturgy as 'a people's way of approaching God in worship; a means of expressing themselves, especially in a congregational setting, before God, and of assuring themselves of communion with Him . . . a means by which human souls finds a link with the living Spirit who is God'.[27]

The liturgies of the Western-established Churches clearly fall short of this definition because they were all imported from the traditions of their home missions. This is why services of worship in them are lifeless, drab, boring and uninspiring. The liturgies become stereotyped, formal, monotonous and absolutely un-related to the African way of worship. The reason for this awful situation is simply that they were not composed from the spiritual, emotional and ritual needs of the people and so have remained essentially alien to Africans. What of the African believer critically following the Anglican minister as he reads his service from an archaic Book of Common Prayer, Sunday in and Sunday out? Or the African worshipper watching the Catholic priest at service, and not even understanding the language he is speaking? By nature, the African wants to be actively involved in the worship of the deity, a dynamic participant. He is not content with being a passive spectator.

The Indigenous Churches are characterised by a greater measure of spontaneity and excitability. Their use of indigenous music is an innovation which accounts for much of their evangelistic achievement. Africans naturally love rhythm and music, and they love to dance, and sing in a way meaningful to them. All these means have been employed by the Indigenous Churches to bring Christianity home to the African within his cultural setting. They composed and sang hymns 'in indigenous idiom and music, with indigenous musical instruments. . . . Naturally such hymns and lyrics struck the right note in the heart. This was the one thing which touched the emotional depths which foreign liturgies could not reach'.[28]

The Indigenous Churches believe in the efficacy of prayers. They always pray vigorously, hardly ever quietly and with the greatest confidence that under normal circumstances their prayers will be answered, if possible spontaneously. They therefore never give up any case as impossible, whatever the contrary evidence. Where prayers are not answered, it is the petitioner's fault. Perhaps he does not have the faith, or he has made no atonement for his previous sins. This faith is largely responsible for their strong belief in divine healing, driving some to the fanatical point of rejecting medicine of any kind. Their standpoint is that whatever we ask God in Jesus' name will be given. Whatever prayer cannot solve must be resigned to the will of God. This is an African approach if we acknowledge the religious basis of the African's very existence.

The whole point of divine healing is that it is an answer to one of the problems which drive the believer back to the traditional religion. The role of the healer is similar to that of the traditional diviner or *babalawo*. The traditional causes of illness are accepted by the Indigenous Churches, especially causes that can be attributed to malignant spiritual powers, witches and implacable enemies. This gives confidence to the patient and with the mutual faith he shares with the healer, the miracle can take place. Whether this is only a temporary relief arising from a psychological situation is not easy to determine, but suffice it to say that these Churches' ministry of healing has contributed greatly to their spectacular evangelistic successes.

In contrast to this is the indifference of the older Churches to the miraculous aspect of healing, and it is therefore their members who in despondency continue to drift in embarrassing numbers to the indigenous Churches for divine healing, and prompted by other spiritual needs. To them, the ministry of healing is in fulfilment of the ministry of Christ, who, after restoring good health to men, showed them the way to God. In other words, the Indigenous Churches saw healing not as an end but as the means to an end, namely faith in God.

Thirdly, manifestations of the Spirit. This is one of the fundamentals that distinguish the Indigenous Churches from other Churches, and it is the reason why they call themselves 'spiritual' Churches. They believe they are always guided by the inspiration of the Holy Spirit. The believer, in total and ascetic submission, hears the Voice of God in dreams, vision, trances and prophecies. This is why dialogues, disputations and logicalities such as are common in the Western-oriented Churches are unknown among them. In visions, dreams, prophecies, etc., it is God who has spoken through his servants. His words cannot be challenged. These phenomena – which, it is believed by

these Churches, characterised the Pentecostal experience – are
still possible in our days. Their absence in the older Churches
has been seen by the Indigenous Churches as symptomatic of
their spiritual sterility. The African is naturally anxious to
know what the future has in store for him – how he can possibly
change a bad destiny, what forces or powers militate against
his endeavours, and how best he can fight them. In the traditional society he went to the diviner for an answer to his
besetting problems. When the missionaries came, they told him
it was idolatry to go to the diviner. He should believe only in
God through Jesus Christ. To the African this is an abstract
faith which only multiplies his problems. This is why he
continues secretly to visit the diviner. But with the emergence
of the Indigenous Churches, he finds in their prophets a most
effective substitute for the traditional divine. Their roles are
fundamentally identical. Here the suppliant finds a Church
ministering to his spiritual and existential needs. It is no longer
that alien Church which failed to see eye to eye with him. As
with the diviner, he is even given concrete objects to aid his
prayers and restore his confidence – holy water, candles,
incense, consecrated oil, psalms to rehearse, Bible passages to
recite. No longer need he go to the diviner: Jesus Christ has
proved that his faith can be given expression from the perspective
of his tradition and culture. This is the essence of the belief in
the charismata of the Spirit. The phenomena of speaking with
tongues and spirit possession would not appear strange to the
African even though these are no longer considered indispensable
in the Church universal – a question which has yet to be settled
in the Church.

A significant point that must not be overlooked is the status
of women in the Indigenous Churches. The positions of women
like Alice Lenshina of Zambia, Grace Tani of Ghana, and
Sophia Odunlami, Christianah Olatunrinle and Captain
Abiodun of Nigeria, not only reflect the Montanist movement
of the early Church which gave positions of authority to women,
but also see a picture of the traditional religion which gave room
to women leaders and priestesses. The rather discriminatory
attitude to women of the Western-related Churches, ostensibly
in obedience to Pauline injunctions, is in matters of religion
quite alien to Africa.

Finally, we need to point to the evangelistic concern of the indigenous Churches. The Christian Church is supposed to be an evangelistic Church (witness the last command of Jesus Christ). This is taken seriously by the Indigenous Churches, which could conveniently have relied on the propaganda-effect of their healing ministry, and the activities of their prophets, but they organise frequent and regular open-air evangelistic campaigns. In this way, new members continue to flock to their Churches even from the other Churches. Statistical evidence continues to reveal a tremendous rise in their membership.

This then is what we have considered as the African expression of Christianity, which has really made it the religion of Africans; the religion that can lead them finally to the realisation of their ultimacy and to the throne of God. The effectiveness of the ministry of these Churches illustrates the fact that God can speak to the Africans in their own language and in their own traditional and cultural setting. It is also a challenge to the other Churches which continue to take refuge in the notion that unless Christianity is practised in the White man's way, it is idolatry and not correct.

Many are the weaknesses and shortcomings of these movements, and they have been ignored here deliberately. This is because it is our discovery of these faults and our positive and objective efforts to rectify them that can rouse us from our stupor and finally lead us to the ultimate goal, so that we shall be able to see Christianity from the perspective of Africa. One fact, however, remains certain: that through these Indigenous Churches Christianity has been implanted in the African milieu, and the spiritual ambivalence of the people has been considerably weakened, making the individual believer an integrated whole.

We can thus conclude that through these Churches Christianity has come to stay in Africa. As the religion of Africans it is never likely to be undermined by any invasion or by the ultimate departure of the Whites who first brought it to the continent.

REFERENCES

1. G. C. Oosthuizen, *Post Christianity in Africa*, London: C. Hurst, 1968, p. xi.
2. Ibid., p. 1.

3. 'Writing African History', *The Church Crossing Frontiers*, Uppsala, pp. 90–108.
4. Paper presented in typescript at the History Post-Graduate Seminar on 'Social and political Aspects of the Donatist Schism in North Africa' on 6 May, 1971.
5. E. A. Ayandele, 'Why Christianity in Africa', paper presented at the History Post-Graduate Seminar on 29 October, 1970.
6. Ibid., p. 3.
7. Ibid.
8. E. B. Idowu, *Towards an Indigenous Church*, London: Oxford University Press, 1965, p. 4.
9. J. F. A. Ajayi, *Christian Missions in Nigeria 1841–1891*, London: Longmans 1965, p. 208.
10. Ibid.
11. Ibid., p. 189.
12. Ibid., p. 188.
13. Ibid., p. 194.
14. Ibid., p. 195.
15. Beetham, *Christianity and the New Africa*, London: Pall Mall Press, 1967, p. 20.
16. Oosthuizen, op. cit., p. xi.
17. Ibid., p. 20.
18. Ibid.
19. E. B. Idowu, '*The Predicament of the Church in Africa*, p. 426.
20. G. Baeta, *Prophetism in Ghana*, London, 1962.
21. Op. cit., p. 11.
22. Ibid.
23. Op. cit.
24. Ajayi and Ayandele, op. cit., p. 12.
25. Ibid., p. 12.
26. H. W. Turner, *Profile Through Preaching*, pp. 8–9.
27. E. B. Idowu, *Towards an Indigenous Church*, p. 26.
28. Ibid., p. 44.

I I

THE THEOLOGICAL MEANING
OF TRUE HUMANITY

by Manas Buthelezi

The category of 'the human' is becoming increasingly important
as a point of reference in current socio-ethical discussions. Among
other things it serves as a common denominator for a wide
spectrum of ethical presuppositions in common discussions
centred on the theme of justice.

Contemporary concerns for 'human rights' and 'human
dignity' stem from man's quest for self-understanding and self-
realisation in the face of dehumanising facets of modern life.
Man's elementary possession in this world is *mutatis mutandis* his
'self'. He has an inalienable right to be himself in the way that
he wants. The right to selfhood is elementary to man's humanity,
and is one with his moral accountability. Yet many a time
man's selfhood is made prisoner in its own human house; he
becomes an object of manipulation by forces – human or
otherwise – that vie to take possession of his selfhood and to
shape and direct it for their own ends. The convicted culprits
in this regard are not only man's sheer inhumanity to man but
also a constellation of social, economic and political factors in
modern life.

Man suddenly discovers his humanity in caricature form: he
realises that he is neither what he thought he was nor what he
would like to be. Out of this mental and emotional torture
arise a number of existential questions: 'After all, who am I?'
'What is the destiny of my being and mode of existence?' 'How
can I so live as to overcome what militates against the realisation
of my destiny as a human being?'

This in essence is the quest for true or authentic humanity.

For a black man such as I am, this issue is loaded with historical accidents which project a peculiar dimension on the basic quest: 'Can I realise my authentic humanity in the medium of my blackness?' Is my blackness some fatalistic road-block in life or a context within which God has made it possible for me to be an authentic man?' The theoteleological aspect of these questions was phrased by the Rev. Ph.· Mthethwa thus: 'But God, why did you create us?'

By true or authentic humanity we do not mean some Platonic abstraction thought to be an 'ideal man', but rather that state and form of existence which God intended when he created man. This immediately raises the problem of the criterion of true humanity and also makes it necessary for us to characterise what is not true humanity.

We shall first discuss what we understand to be the basic theological criteria for authentic humanity. We shall only touch on the problem of the image of God in man as well as man's status as a redeemed creature of God. In the second main section we will deal with the 'existential contradictions' in the realisation of true humanity.

(i) *Some Theological Criteria of True Humanity*

I. MAN AS CREATED IN THE IMAGE OF GOD

The Old Testament uses the phrase 'image and likeness' to describe the truth of man's unique creaturely relatedness to God (Gen. 1: 26). Even though the textual context does not explain the phrase. and rather more concerns what is implied by man being the image of God, one is still able to infer that the unique dignity of man's relatedness to God is intended and expressed. The author of Genesis (Gen. 2: 7) wants to portray man as one who has dominion over all the rest of God's creatures. Man is a representative of God in the world, standing and acting in God's stead.

As an aspect of man's creaturely relation to God, this expression 'divine image and likeness' is not primarily definitive of an ontological quality in man seen in himself, but rather describes the unique and dynamic relationship which exists between God, creator, and man, creature. Man is not *the* image of God, but he *was created in God's image*. About this Irenaeus says:

Man is created in the image of God, and the image of God is the Son, in whose image man was created. For this reason the Son also appeared in the fullness of time to show how the copy resembles Him.

Attempts have been made in the past to embrace the concept of 'image and likeness' in ontological categories. Thomas Aquinas tried to understand this within the framework of his theory of being. Thus he was able to undertake the formation of the hierarchical ordering of being according to the proportionality which each grade of being involves. The theory of the analogy of being is the *via media* of Thomas Aquinas for escaping the philosophical extremes of monism and pluralism of being. He thus develops the view that all created things show forth the image of God in a certain degree. The infinite nature of God is a being which has existence of itself. While a finite thing is also a being, it is a being from another; it is a caused being. Hence it follows that some things are like God first inasmuch as they exist; others inasmuch as they have life, and a third class inasmuch as they have mind or intelligence. Those which have intelligence approach nearer to God than any other creatures. Thus, properly speaking, intellectual creatures alone are made in God's image. It is in this special analogical way that man is the unique being created in the image of God.

Thomas, in various places, develops a theory of causality which grounds the ontology of creatures in their Creator. The somewhat mechanical chain of causality is evident in Thomas' attempt to explain the relationship between the image and the exemplar:

Every agent is found to produce effects which resemble it. Hence if the first goodness is the efficient cause of all good things, it must imprint its likeness upon the things which it produces.

The analogical relationship between the creature and the Creator is also understood in terms of participation. 'Since God is existence itself, each thing participates in a likeness of God in as much as it exists'. Aquinas is careful to warn that this relationship between the Creator and the creature is by no means reducible to a 'community of univocation', but is a 'community of analogy'. In other words, 'the creature is not

said to be similar to God as though God participated in the
same form which the creature shared. Rather the reason is
that God is the very form substantially, while the creature
participates in this form through a kind of imitation.' Here
Thomas is rejecting any notion of analogy of participation which
would imply even analogously that both God and creatures
are sharing in some *tertium quid* that is prior to both of them as a
medium of participation. Hence Thomas' hierarchical ontological pyramid in which God is the ultimate being in whom all
other beings participate:

> Since all things which are participate in existence and are
> being by participation, there must necessarily be a being at
> the summit of all things who is existence by his very essence,
> whose essence is identical with his existence. This being is
> God, the sufficient, most honourable, and perfect cause of all
> existence, from whom all things that are participate in being.

In Luther, however, we see an entirely different approach,
not only because he belongs to the Platonist-Augustinian
philosophical tradition, but also because his thought is informed
by creational, rather than ontological motifs. To align Luther
with the Platonist tradition may be misleading. Therefore this
needs some qualification. Here we mean nothing more than the
element of dualism which is manifest in his writings. Terms
like 'visible' and 'invisible', 'sensible' and 'insensible', 'image'
and 'exemplar' suggest an ultimate philosophical origin. This
is especially the case in his commentary on the Psalms, as F.
Edward Cranz has observed:

> The form of Luther's theology in the Dictate is transitional
> from a philosophical theology (or a theological philosophy)
> to a new theology of the cross which is contrasted with a
> philosophy of appearances. The philosophical theology may
> with qualification be described as Platonist, and it centres on
> such concepts as image and exemplar, visible and invisible.

The dualism remains, but there is a shift from ontological to
Biblical motifs. This is true even though in the early Luther,
especially, the philosophical terminology is still retained. For
instance, Christ is represented as both figure and exemplar,
and his humanity is the 'sign in which all things were signified',
while the glorified Christ is the 'thing signified by all things'.

Luther therefore remarks: 'Christ is the goal of all things and their centre, towards whom all look and towards whom all point, as if they said: "Behold, He is the one who *is*, while we *are not*, but simply signify." ' Gradually, however, there is a shift from what is a matter of 'analogy' and 'proportion' to the matter of opposites. He speaks of God as giving his eternal good under their opposites and 'He makes the sign contradict the thing signified.'

At this point we should return to our main topic. When Luther discusses the image of God in which man was created, his whole approach is religious. He confesses that, after the Fall of man, it is impossible to reconstruct this image. In his critique of the speculations of the Fathers, he adds: 'When we speak about that image, we are speaking about something unknown. Not only have we had no experience of it, but we continually experience the opposite; and so we hear nothing but bare words'.

Luther does not attempt to isolate the conception of the image from the totality of man in his relatedness to God. He maintains that the entire image of God was impressed upon man in his creation in such a way that it belonged to his essential nature of creatureliness. It was not something which was added to the being of man. Luther is reacting against the Augustinian and Scholastic theology which taught, among other things, that 'it was only the elements of the image which belonged to the essential nature of Adam, and Adam received all else as a gift over and above his natural endowments, either immediately or at a later moment.'

Luther does not distinguish between man's original state in which man had the image of God and original righteousness. According to him the two coincide. Of the verse 'Let him have dominion over the fish of the sea' Luther points out that this 'dominion' is a form of God's delegated authority as an aspect of the divine image of man. Through the Fall man forfeited the brilliance of God's image in him. Yet this did not reduce him to the level of the brute. It is the fact of having been created in the likeness of God that accounts for man's humanity.

Even as a sinner, man has not crossed the boundary between the human and the brute. To be sure, he often behaves like a brute and sometimes adopts the law of the jungle for regulating his relations and dealings with other men. As a sinner he is redeemable, because he is man: he is man because he was created in the image of God. To be sure, he can be denied the right to live as man when he becomes victim to the sinful brutality of other men who have adopted the moral code of the jungle in their relation towards him. The historical institution of slavery and racial animosity are classic examples of man in his brutal sinfulness adopting the moral code of the jungle as the norm for regulating his relations with his fellow-men. Even as a slave and when radically oppressed, man has always been redeemable from the social consequences of sin. He is redeemable because he was created in the image of God. This leads us to our next section.

2. MAN AS A REDEEMED CREATURE OF GOD

In 1 Cor. 5: 17 Paul uses 'new creation' to describe the renewal and transformation of the individual in Christ. The starting-point for this anthropological process is God's grace of forgiveness which man receives in baptism. Through baptism man becomes a member of the community of forgiven sinners and is invested with the potentiality of growth in this grace. In the process of growth and renewal he is nurtured by the Word and sacraments. According to Paul, baptism places man in a position of solidarity with Christ. In Rom. 6: 1–14 Paul maintains that 'in the act of baptism the baptised man enters upon fellowship with Christ, and in such a manner that he gains a participation in Christ's death and resurrection'.

The phenomena of dying and rising with Christ are possible only in created life. The baptismal New Life is transmitted through created things which belong to the life of everyday: water, linguistic forms and human agents. Just as God does not wave a wand – to use Luther's expression – in bringing children into the world, but uses men and women, so he gives man new life, not through the medium of some unfamiliar hocus-pocus, but by using what is there in the structure of human existence. It thus follows that the integrity of God's grace is not exclusive of the mundane created things which are used for mediating that grace.

If redemption puts man on the road towards the realisation of his true humanity in Christ, this can obviously take place only in the medium of daily life. Man does not wait to be transformed into a new man in heaven; it takes place here on earth.

This then raises a number of practical questions which will serve to introduce us to the next main section: Can the Christian reach his full potential as man if he lives under sub-human conditions such as poverty, slavery and other humiliations? If not, does this mean that some people will realise their authentic humanity as redeemed creatures of God only in heaven and not while they live as Christians in this world? Is this really God's basic redemption plan for us?

(ii) An Analysis of Existential Contradictions in the Realisation of True Humanity

1. AN UNDERSTANDING OF THE WHOLENESS OF LIFE

It has been rightly said that the African has a sense of the wholeness of life. The traditional African religion was characterised by the wholeness of life; it is even more correct to say that religion and life belonged together. Far from being a department of life, religion was life. As a result of this it lacked institutional symbols which would have marked it off from daily life. There was no separate community of religious people because everyone who participated in the life of the community also participated in its religion.

The continuity of fellowship between the living and the dead was analogous to the interplay between the supernatural and natural worlds. Life was so much a whole that not even death could disintegrate it. Thus death was not regarded as a point which marked the termination of fellowship among those who had been in communion on this side of the grave. This solidarity between the living and the dead was possible because of the active presence of the Creator of Life, from whose presence neither the living nor the dead could escape. His presence was an existential experience on the part of man. The validity of this presence did not depend on the extent to which it was conceptualised. In other words it was as one participated in life that one apprehended God's presence.

Adeolu Adegobola has vividly described how historical Christianity was insensitive towards this African insight. I shall quote him at length:

This warping of Christian thought in Africa concerning the relation of God to the world is in opposition to the biblical insight of our day and to the best traditions of the people of Africa. Man in traditional African society never separated the sacred from the secular as he was later taught to do. The routine of daily life, the momentous crises of human experience, both individual and public affairs, have all been seen as realms over which the almighty reigned supreme. Unfortunately, conversion to Christianity has meant, among other things, acceptance of the view that life can be divided into spiritual and material, worldly and heavenly; and God has been thought of as being in control only of the spiritual. Society has been viewed as if it were only in the control of man. Catechumens have been led to repeat the Apostles' Creed, 'God the Father Almighty, Maker of heaven and earth,' and at the same time to behave as if the earth were outside God's sovereign control and better left in the hands of the 'princes of this world'.

It is impossible to grasp this concept of the wholeness of life if one does not take seriously the fact that God is the Creator of all things. Indeed, there may be various forms of corporate life, like church and world, but these forms of life are always *coram Deo*.

The concept of the wholeness of life is important not just because it happens to reflect a traditional African insight, but more so because it serves to preserve the integrity of man. This leads us to the next point.

2. REALITY OF ALIENATION FROM THE WHOLENESS OF LIFE

The problem of alienation engulfs the black man in South Africa with its deadly tentacles. Alienation and the realisation of true humanity are mutually exclusive concepts. The Christian understanding of man has yet to be translated into the practical reality of the black man.

In the light of the Christian faith, man at his creation was given dominion over the rest of creation. Hence his status as man entailed sharing in the governance of creation under God. Redemption from sin includes the restoration of this dignity of man in creation. The open question is what relevance this has for the black man.

When we speak of an authentic man, we are not thinking of

one with a 'colonised' humanity, who is the object of 'dominion' by other men, but of one with a 'post-colonial' humanity, that is one who has been redeemed to share with others the God-given 'dominion' over creation. By 'colonised humanity' we mean a state of existence in which the selfhood is crushed by external factors and circumstances or is subject to pressure from outside to direct itself in such a way as to serve interests other than those of self. The extreme example of 'colonised humanity' is found in conditions of slavery. We may also define 'colonised humanity' as a state of existence in which the selfhood becomes alienated from its 'human house'. The selfhood is placed under 'house arrest'.

Historical factors have caused the African to develop a '*masochistic complex*', that is, the realisation of personal fulfilment in unconscious self-hatred and the despising and loathing of everything with which the ego is identified in social and cultural life. The degree to which one is ready to go through this psychic mortification virtually becomes the criterion for ascertaining the level which one has reached in the realisation of the image of a 'civilised and Christian man'. The point of the orientation of the ego becomes the outside father-image of a missionary or 'Westerner'. It is easy to confuse this psychological inversion and depersonalisation with conversion and sanctification. The social counterpart of this inversion has been the bourgeois socio-cultural Church life pattern around the mission station.

At worst, the black man has to bow to opinions and ideas of those whom he has been conditioned to associate with authority and enlightenment. At best, he has only to choose between those alternatives which are offered to him. The consequence of this is that his mind has become a channel, rather than a fountain of ideas, even in those things which regulate and are decisive for his daily life.

Writing about the problem of cultural change, Bronislaw Malinowski has referred to another expression of alienation from the wholeness of life in what he calls 'selective giving'. He discusses the imbalance between what the African has lost and what he has received of Western culture. Although he is writing on the basis of the situation before the end of the Second World War, his observations serve to explain a number of riddles in present everyday life.

The Europeans have given schools, medical services, and they have also tried to evangelise the natives. In some way they have given the African a more effective administration; they have opened up the continent with a set of roads, railways and airways. The African is to a certain extent allowed to benefit by some of these advantages of a more highly developed civilisation. But in assessing the value of the things given as against those taken away, we must not forget that, when it comes to spiritual gifts, it is easy to give but difficult to accept. Material advantages, on the other hand, are easily accepted but only relinquished with reluctance. Yet it is just the spiritual gifts with which we are most generous, while we withhold wealth, power, independence and social equality. Even when it comes to spiritual gifts, we often hand out the shadow and not the substance. . . . We also give him advice in the form of our religion. At times this is so Puritanical and high-pitched in its ideals as to lead the native into hypocrisy and to divorce him from the ordinary pleasures of his tribal life.

Malinowski goes on to point out that this selective giving and withholding is both significant and determined. It is the withdrawal from culture contact of all those elements which make up the full benefits – economic, political and legal – of the higher culture. If power, wealth and social amenities were given, culture change would be a comparatively easy and smooth process.

The naked truth is that the African Christian lives at the fringe of life. He has been a victim of selective giving and withholding. He has not been allowed to realise the potential of his humanity. In other words he has become alienated from that wholeness of life which in his religious tradition helped him not to live as a split personality. As we said earlier, in his religious tradition the 'ideal' was not a conceptualised reality but a reality realised in the very particpation of life itself. The Western mind can live with a discrepancy between the 'ideal' and the 'real', because the 'ideal' can exist as a conceptualisation.

That is why the Christian conscience has been able to live and even to have the power to condone such evil de-humanising social institutions as slavery and the oppression of man by man. The Christian conscience of the Western tradition has always found the way out by abstracting the 'ideal' from the 'real'. It gets its peace of mind in such arguments as: 'If only everybody were a Christian at heart you would not have all these problems'. The 'Christian at heart' is, of course, the 'ideal Christian' who stands compared to the 'real Christian' whom we meet every day. When shall the 'ideal' Christian come to meet us? If certain conditions in life militate against man's realisation of true humanity, the 'Christian ideal' is certainly called in question, because the true humanity of some people may be at stake. To continue speaking of 'brotherhood in Christ' while there is none in the Christian community in the world may not pose the same problem to the Western mind as it does to the African, who has traditionally believed in the wholeness of life and the reconciliation of 'the real' with 'the ideal' through participation in life itself. How long shall the black Christian wait before he realises true humanity which the gospel has promised him?

I 2

BLACK PEOPLE AND WHITE WORSHIP

by Mongameli Mabona

The question of what worship is and what role it plays in the life of man has not been settled satisfactorily, and because it seems to concern the total human condition, I doubt if it ever will be. The reason for my raising it here is my hope that by thinking on it together we may discover new aspects and gain new insights into this interesting but inexhaustible field of inquiry. It has seemed reasonable to me that I should raise this question before proceeding to consider the relevance of present Christian worship to the life and interests of black people.

It seems to me impossible that anyone whose faith does not include an eschatological dimension can find any meaning and relevance in worship. For my purposes here I will take eschatology and transcendence as parallel terms. Therefore I hold myself to mean by the above statements that anyone who does not believe in a transcendent deity and in the reality of the eternal kingdom cannot worship in a Christian sense. But it is precisely here that we experience the most intractable difficulties with the concept and practice of worship or liturgy.

How can we, a generation surrounded by man-created scientific wonders, with vistas opening up for the ultimate mastery of cosmic processes – how can we be impressed by metaphysical ideas of transcendent beings which are not very apparent? In centuries past the names and presences of transcendent beings were 'immediately felt' by man because man's position in nature was so fragile and vulnerable that he appealed to these transcendent forces at every turn of his life – perhaps several times a day. Today we encourage people to build bigger dams and practice desalination of sea water instead of praying

for rain. There is less and less mention of transcendent beings
in our daily life, and the reason is not the naughtiness of modern
man, but his conquest of the environment. There is no inherent
reason why man should not be able in the long run to manage
all by himself in his environment without the need for appeal-
ing to external forces.

But again, was this prayer addressed to the 'God of the gaps',*
this God who only fills up ultimate human ignorance or ultimate human impotence. This God who was postulated as
'prime mover' by philosophers like Aristotle – was it ever a
Christian one? The idea of 'prime mover' itself is based on
primitive physics which proclaimed that bodies move only
when moved, whereas we know from modern physics that all
bodies continue in uniform motion unless they are stopped.
The 'God of the gaps' is meaningless or will ultimately become
meaningless. And such ideas as 'prime mover' are as unaccept-
able as the Cartesian idea of the point from which the whole
universe has its dynamism, or the Teilhardian idea of Point
Omega.

The God of Christian worship is a personal living and loving
God, not a metaphysical or mathematical abstraction. He is
the God who sent Jesus Christ to us and poured out His Spirit
upon us. His transcendence over us is that of superiority and
not of metaphysical or mathematical infinity. The peoples of
the universe are his family, and this is the inheritance of the
kingdom to which he calls us through Christ.

The liturgy seems to me an expression of family relationships
with a cosmic dimension. I know this explanation will be considered very incomplete because the liturgy is supposed to
penetrate beyond the portals of death. Again I get the impression that our primitive concept of death makes us give to it
a meaning and importance out of all proportion. After all
what shall we think of death when we have become capable
of rousing individuals after they have been deep-frozen for
decades, perhaps for centuries and millenia? The rousing of
Christ from death showed us that death is something very
marginal in human existence.

I think it is clear that I agree fully with those who say that

* Phrase made famous by Professor Coulson, meaning that it is dangerous
to fill in the gaps in our knowledge with a 'God-hypothesis'.

liturgy or worship is a function of life. 'Worship is faith, action, suffering.' Worship is not a 'stepping out of the world'. 'Therefore those elements of worship which promote an authentic relation to reality, such as intercession, offertory, experience of active fellowship and so on, are to be emphasised.'

Moreover in order that reality may remain real to us, it must not be pressed in mysterious or mystifying symbols. We recognise the necessity for symbols in human life: not symbols as mysterious signs but symbols as natural and encompassing expressions of reality. We are not advocating that liturgy should be deprived of all historical dimensions. We are however strongly suggesting that it should always be relevant to life. Mysterious signs and ritualistic gestures are not always an aid in this direction. I maintain that the emphasis in our worship on these latter elements is not Christian but our own, derived from the practices of traditional religions.

Christ's doctrine stresses the reality of God as father of all in the universe, the father who has sent Jesus to us on this earth to teach and save us, the father who has sent us the Holy Spirit to continue Christ's work among us after his departure from this earth. These are the things we are supposed to celebrate in Christian worship and not some mysterious religious or metaphysical realities. We have to get some natural, encompassing expressions for the realities of our fellowship with God and with all human beings in the universe, of our feelings of gratitude for Christ's work among us, of our constant desire for the gift of the Spirit who strengthens us and makes us grow inevitably towards the fulfilment of our comprehensive destiny.

This is the concept of worship with which black people will have to prime themselves. Present so-called Christian worship is full of mysterious signs and mystifying ritualistic gestures by which it tries to communicate with transcendent religious realities. This kind of worship is not progressive – i.e. does not tend towards the fulfilment of true human destiny – but is regressive. To go back to it is worse than useless; it is harmful. We black people have much to catch up with as it is, However, I am not advocating a mass exodus from the existing Christian ecclesiastical communities. If we cannot immediately do away with their forms of worship, let us on our own try to change them by questioning and challenging them at every turn and every opportunity.

Why are forms of Christian worship so stilted and restrained? Are we in worship communicating with an aristocratic or a capitalistic God who wants the little people to be very well behaved or even muted when they approach his majesty? Let there be less cringing and scraping in liturgy. Let us be apostles of more freedom and spontaneity in worship. Why should we have to cringe and scrape even in our father's house? Why the awkward gap between people and ministers? Sometimes the attitude of the assembly towards the president and ministers is like that of the crowd towards an emperor and his retinue. Let there be no participators and spectators in our worship. We are all participators in God's bounty and spectators of his works of loving kindness.

Do we need the type of meditation and spiritual training that is being used in our seminaries and convents? I put this question because attitudes developed in so-called spiritual training come to the surface in the liturgy. I mean the type of meditation in which one is supposed to go into oneself to exercise one's memory, one's imagination and one's sentiments, especially in trying to call up scenes from the life of Jesus and then trying to express one's sentiments about all this. Now, this is supposed to be the kind of exercise that helps to increase one's moral excellence, one's spiritual perfection; for my part, I think this kind of practice to be foreign to our traditions.

I cannot remember in any of the traditional practices of the black people that anyone was encouraged to cultivate high moral excellence or self-perfection by 'entering into himself'. A sensible person in our society was supposed to be one who knew and performed his or her duties towards ancestors and members of the community. The faithful performance of these duties and the development of correct attitudes also towards natural objects was not supposed to imbue such a person with any kind of halo of sanctity or holiness. It was supposed to make him a sensible and well-adjusted member of society and the universe.

Since spirituality is a basic element in our worship, I would advocate that black people should also question and challenge the traditional methods and aims of present spirituality. We do not believe that withdrawal into self can result in any kind of moral excellence, sanctity or holiness, or whatever you call it. We believe in developing correct attitudes towards things and towards men. These pave the way towards fuller communion between the individual and nature and human society. This fuller communion is in itself a healthy state and not any kind of mysterious sanctity or holiness.

Black people have a long way to go. They need to have their senses together and not go chasing after mirages or mares' nests. Let us go on and try to find natural, encompassing expressions for the relationships expressed in worship and spirituality. We are not supermen. We will not find them today or tomorrow. But if we keep on vexing the present situation we are likely to be successful in the long run. By no means, however, should we be misled by mystifying symbols or shimmering expectations.

13

THE CONCEPT OF THE CHURCH
IN BLACK THEOLOGY

by Sabelo Ntwasa

The Church in Historical and Social Perspective

When the first missionaries landed in our country to 'chris-
tianise' the 'savages', they came as part and parcel of a land-
hungry colonialisation surge by their own colonial government. It is in this context that we must view the whole chris-
tianisation and ultimately colonialisation process that has
landed the black man where he is today.

There are two types of missionaries who landed on our
shores: the van der Kempt type,* who wanted Christianity
to adapt itself to the everyday life of the black community,
and the Robert Moffat and Ayliff type, who felt that the whole
life-style of the indigenous community had to be altered to
suit the so-called 'Christian way of life'. Now, the fact that the
latter prevailed was no accident at all.

Now for me, the essential tenets of Christianity are that
Christ was born, that He is the Son of God, and that He came
to redeem mankind. If this so, why should what you wear to
church or the number of wives you have matter? That these
peripheral issues were what the early missionaries made the
central point in the whole Christ-event leaves me aghast.

Let us briefly consider the spread of the Christian message
in England. When St. Augustine and his followers arrived in
England, they found a certain social order predominant. They
preached the good news of the Christ-event, and soon after-
wards England was highly christianised. Later, however,
as the true Englishman saw the conflict that was about to tear
the beloved Motherland in half, namely the well-known 'Royal

* Early nineteenth-century missionary, a protagonist in the emanicipation
of the slaves, which led to the Great Trek.

Divorce', in which the conflict was essentially political ('Is the Pope or the King Head of the English Church?'), the people and their leaders immediately closed ranks behind their king and country, for to them there was no conflict between being a Christian and being a patriot. They were not going to surrender their place in history as a nation to some remote pope in Italy who claimed almost despotic powers over them. Hence the Church of England was established and none can claim that it is less Christian than the Church in France or anywhere else.

But let us return to our own Church here in South Africa. True to the wishes of its white founders, it is essentially the most colonial institution in the country today. Although the membership is almost 70 per cent black, the power and decision-making are still safely in the hands of the white minority. Its liturgy is still essentially Western and white-oriented. All land owned by the Church is registered as white land. Why should this be so in an institution which claims to reject discrimination along racial lines? – for in Christ there is neither Jew nor Greek; neither male nor female. This epitomises the unbridgeable discrepancy between word and action in our white-dominated churches.

Let us briefly consider the liturgy enacted in these churches in South Africa today. We all know that on Sundays we have the Western set form of liturgy, deviation from which is not tolerated in most of our established churches. But on Thursdays and other weekdays we have our '*Izimvusilelo*'* and '*Imijikelezo*'† which ring so true to the African soul that if we stopped them completely we would be in trouble with our mothers. But why are the latter not part of our Sunday services in most of our established churches? I suspect that their black spontaneity and warmth would not be understood by white liturgical experts, who not only tell us where to live and whom to marry but also have the audacity to tell the black man how to pray.

What does this mean to us? Simply that black people in our country have largely resigned themselves to the fate of having other people decide what is good for them. But the worst thing they have done to themselves has been to reject their

* Evangelical revival services.
† Going about the streets inviting people to religious services.

traditional form of expression, even in their own liturgy, and exalt the white man and Western styles of worship which for me means only one thing: that the predominance of white value systems in the Church life of the black man has led him to equate whiteness with value and so to aspire to be white.

Now this is a cardinal sin, for the intricate relationship between societal value and credal values in Christianity was deliberately established by the white authors of colonialist Christianity, not only to introduce Christianity, but also to supplant the existing societal order. Wherever they set foot the black people have consistently turned away from themselves and their blackness, seeking to emulate whites, thereby going against the deliberate plan of whomever created them black. The adaptability of the Christian religion shows very well that its universality does not imply uniformity, yet anyone who wants to deny his own self (e.g. his blackness) in favour of another (whiteness) is sinning in the eyes of his creator, and since we agree that God created him, his sin is a direct insult to the intelligence and integrity of Christ our Brother and of God our Father.

Now traditional Christianity, as taught us by our know-all white tutors, has set out to teach us a lot about our shortcomings and little about the positive and essentially good nature of man. Thus the black man in South Africa is a paranoid creature, spending most of his time paying libations to an angry God who seeks to be appeased at all costs. He thus forgets his essential 'God-likeness' which is what the Christ-event is about and what it asserts. This negative concentration on the individual removes us from the essential factor of interdependence in society, and makes us seek to solve individually the problems that accrue from our joint situation. This concentration on the spiritual dimension of man acts as the exclusion of his physical dimension. The black man's response to God is daily tampered with by the *physical* factors surrounding him – his poverty, his separation from his wife and children because of migratory labour laws, constant insults to his human dignity, constant exposure to corruption, disease, etc. – all of which are results of the socio-political system governing him and his kind.

Thus any religion, to be meaningful to him, has to take

cognisance of his socio-political situation and the need for him to respond in unity with his kind to this political situation in a self-protective manner. For it is only when the physical obstacles in the way between God and man are removed that man can fully realise his spiritual dimension. This constant need for people to care for the human body is almost a command from God. As Mahatma Gandhi so aptly put it:

> All religions agree in regarding the human body as an abode of God. Our body has been given to us on the understanding that we should render devoted service to God with its aid. It is our duty to keep it pure and unstained from within as well as from without, so as to render it back to its Giver, when the time comes for it, in the state of purity in which we got it.

This is why some of us who see Christ in *our* perspective, our black perspective in the South African scene, know that our Saviour would not cry out in the familiar words he is said to have uttered so many centuries ago – 'Man shall not live by bread alone, but by every word that comes from the Word of God' – and mean that we should not be interested in bread, for he knows only too well that Man can not live by the Word of God alone, but must have bread as well. We must also remember that the individualistic approach of the missionaries is due to their having come from an individualistic society; hence their failure to understand our communal- and man-centred society, which is the hallmark of the black world.

This is where the case for Black Theology begins. For as long as the black man sits on his laurels, waiting for definitions of the Christ-event by others, he will remain in his present condition as a third-rate person, little more than a labour unit. Black Theology calls to black churchmen to start defining the Christ-event for themselves and to stop waiting for others to do it for them. Black Theology describes Christ as a fighting God, not a passive God who allows a lie to exist unchallenged. Black Theology grapples with existential problems and does not claim to be a theology of absolutes. It seeks to return God to the black man and to the truth and reality of his situation. This is an important aspect of Black Consciousness, for quite a large proportion of the black population are still wallowing in the mire of confusion, the aftermath of the missionary epoch. It is therefore the duty of all black priests and ministers of religion to take on themselves the task of saving, by adopting the Black Theology approach and thereby once more uniting the black man to his God.

And all the white, imbibed values in our life-style as black people will never die unless my brothers will sit up and heed the call of Black Theology and just for a moment forget the vulgar fish-and-chips and coca-cola way of life we have inherited from the white world. The words of a remarkable black woman poet come to mind here:

Will the real black people please stand,
Moved towards their own blackness,
Prone to influence and set trends,
Schooled in their times and folkways,
Dedicated to worthwhile endeavours,
Attentive to meaningful expression.

The Church in Theological Perspective

Throughout the first half of this paper we have spoken of 'the Christ-event'. We now need to ask: What is the relationship between the Christ-event and the Church?' We have argued that the essential tenet of Christianity is the acceptance of Christ as redeemer. What are we to understand by redemption?

The most common understanding of this, expecially since Martin Luther, has been that by faith alone is a person forgiven, acquitted and accepted. Along with this it has been argued that Christ came to arouse faith in himself, and through himself to give access to God. Consequently the Church has been seen primarily as an organisation of people who have come to faith in Christ: the chief mark of the Church has been its profession of faith. But it would seem that this represents an inadequate understanding of redemption, and fails to do justice to the New Testament teaching.

In the first place, in his famous teaching in Romans 6, Paul speaks of dying and rising *with* Christ. In Western Christianity this teaching has largely been divorced from Paul's Hebrew philosophy: it has been spiritualised to an emotional oneness with Christ, a spiritual experience of Christ. In this form it has been the backbone of the highly emotional Billy Graham type of evangelism.

But to understand what Paul says more adequately we need to take into account his Hebrew background and especially the Hebrew concept of time. Time for the Hebrew was not perceived as a long-drawn-out series of events with past, present and future clearly demarcated. Rather, as was so typical of the Hebrews, time had a psychic quality; it was felt, and felt in its quality. An event was thought of as 'past' only if it was felt to have no more significance; even if it happened centuries before, it was felt to belong to the present insofar as its reality was still a present experience. Thus we get what Kierkegaard called the sense of contemporaneity. Present and past became fused in the shared quality of the present and the past event. We, who tend to think of events as something external to ourselves, might call these two events separated in time. The Hebrews, who tended to think of events as felt realities, and being unable to distinguish between the felt responses to the events, would fuse them into one continuing event.

With this background we can return to Paul's 'dying and rising *with* Christ' with new insight. Christ's death was an event. But for Paul that death had the quality and significance of being a death in which Christ's struggle against evil or Satan in his life now entered into its decisive phase. Here Christ entered into his last and most bitter struggle against 'the enemy' and overcame him, and the resurrection was the outcome of this victory and bore witness to this victory.

Thus, for the Christian, to 'die *with* Christ' is not to have a 'spiritual experience' of Christ, but so to fuse his life with Christ's that it takes on the quality of Christ's life and death. It is to become contemporaneous with Christ in the sense of a perceived quality. It is therefore to share the quality of being totally engaged in the struggle against evil – against people's bonds. It is to be involved in the same on-going struggle in which Christ was involved. The Church therefore cannot be seen simply as the company of believers who have had spiritual experiences. It is the company of those whose lives are perceived to have the quality of Christ-in-his-struggle-against-human-bondage. It is thus the company of liberators, or it is not the Church.

This also is the meaning of Paul's favourite phrase of being 'in Christ'. It does not mean being in a 'spiritual unity' with Christ, just as when the Old Testament speaks of being 'in David' it does not mean having a spiritual relationship with David. Being 'in David' means bearing so much of the character of David that a person would think he was meeting David himself. So being 'in Christ' means having Christ's quality of life. So all of these great expressions of Paul point to a quality of life – i.e. sharing Christ's quality which was setting people free.

In Black Theology this means on the one hand accepting that racism of white against black is an intolerable bondage to the blacks, and thus becoming involved in a life of action to set people free from this bondage. Therefore, Black Theology must affirm that the Church is that company of people who 'die with Christ' in the quality of life which is totally committed to liberating black people.

But we must follow Paul's logic still further. If past and present are made one in the shared quality of the events, then it is the quality of the corporate life which constitutes its unity. This is the basis of Paul's argument for the unity of the Church. As he says so powerfully in 1 Corinthians 1, if two people are united with Christ, then they must be one and cannot be divided, and if they are divided then they cannot both be united with Christ. Thus Paul's favourite image of the Church is that of a single human body, which may have many different organs all serving different vital functions, but completely united. But in saying this Paul has two things in mind: on the one hand there is the felt and perceived dynamic unity with Christ (Paul calls him the body's head), which means total involvement in his work of liberation, and on the other, and equally important, there is the felt and perceived dynamic unity with each other, which means feeling our lives bound up with each other in the dynamic of liberation.

Paul explains his meaning in very practical terms in 1 Corinthians 11 when he deals with the bad behaviour of the Corinthians at the Lord's Supper. He makes it clear that the object of his attack is the way the wealthy Corinthians always arrive early and gobble up all the food and drink before the poor slaves arrive and find they have nothing. This, he says, makes it impossible to eat the Lord's Supper (v. 20), because they have failed to 'discern the body', which 'body' he links both with the bread (v. 24) and with 'ourselves' (v. 31). Thus he sees Christ and the community of Christians as one dynamic unity – and if ever that unity is disrupted by thoughtless, greedy, or unkind behaviour, not only do the poor suffer but Christ is so betrayed as to turn the Eucharist into a farce.

This means that we have to add to what we have said of individuals bearing the liberating quality of Christ's life. We have to add the extra essential of an absolutely binding sense of unity so that the whole bears a single quality – liberation. If anything splits that dynamic unity, then Christ is so divided that that which calls itself 'Church' must be something else. In Black Theology, the Church is that company of people who 'die with Christ' in the quality of life which is totally committed to liberating black people – and among whom there are such strong bonds that they would rather die than humiliate or accept the humiliation or indignity of any brother. It is thus that company of people whose total corporate life and action is black unity for black liberation. To be for liberation is not enough; that is not the Church. Absolutely indispensable is a profoundly and deeply *desired* and *experienced* sense of black unity. And unity is not enough. We have in South Africa enough white unity and to spare. But it is unity for the domination of blacks not their liberation.

We have seen above how individualistic and racist what calls itself the Church in South Africa is and has been. This in itself is reason enough for black Christians to create a black Church. But, more than this, blacks know within themselves the foreignness of individualism in Africa. However much we have been infected by it there is deeply embedded within our black culture and society a sense of oneness, called by Wheeler Robinson 'corporate personality'. This non-individualism blacks need to claim with pride and attempt to translate it into the life-style of the Christian Church. We need to do this not simply because it is our black thing, but also because it is so profoundly close to the New Testament basis of the Christian Church.

Conclusion

Let us finally anticipate the question: 'What about whitey'? Are whites to be excluded because they are not black, a physical fact about which they can do nothing? The answer must be yes. Blacks have suffered under white rule, including white rule in the Church, for too long. We have not only suffered under white rule, but we have been fragmented by our white tutors, who have painted the great Christian ideal as individualistic piety. Perhaps they could do no other, coming to Christianity as they have with their Western background of capitalistic individualism. As a result all they have been able to do is to add 'faith in Christ' to their unchanged individualism. And to this individualism they have tried to convert blacks.

This has to be rejected totally. Individualists cannot be concerned about liberation. Blacks, therefore, with their tremendous sense of community in their culture, have the responsibility of building this into the very fabric of the life of the Church. To do this they cannot depend on the leadership or guidance of whites. Even the most radical of whites can only dream of the sense of community that is in the marrow and blood of blacks.

Thus blacks must take the lead, a lead from which our blackness debars us in the white-controlled churches. For the sake of the Church, therefore, we must do it. Then, having done it, we will have the responsibility of bringing the Gospel to the white man. We will have the responsibility of offering him the joy of belonging to a community which is marked by a known and felt unity in the dynamic corporate life which surges on to break every yoke of human bondage.

This should not be seen as a plea for black ecumenism. Ecumenism is the white man's superficial thing. As we have come to know it, it is an endless round of debates by white churchmen in an attempt to break down the structural divisions in the Church by reaching some agreed confessional formula. As such it remains white-dominated, individualistic and verbal. Our need is way out beyond this. It is a unity in total commitment to each other in a corporate life 'in Christ', a life of action which has liberation as its goal. This will be our black

Church – a black unity in total commitment to every black person in a corporate black life 'in Christ' for black liberation. It will carry within itself the seed of hope for any white man whose heart can be moved.

14

BLACK THEOLOGY AND AUTHORITY

by Mokgethi Motlhabi

Power and Racism

Perhaps one of the most distressing aspects of almost every organisation in South Africa which is committed in some way to eradicate racism is the shallow analysis made of racism. Both religious and secular bodies have set up various committees to combat racism, for which large sums of money have been set aside. There are some analysts who do not see racism as the kernel of the evil in our society, but they are few and far between.

It should be clear that a frontal attack on racism, even if it were to succeed, would change society very little. Racism is a prejudice. But no socially significant prejudice exists simply because people are inherently prone to prejudices. The truth is much more that on some easily identifiable differences between people – which is a natural focus for prejudice – a myth is created. These myths are not stupid or unreasonable, but serve very important social functions. The more successfully they serve the social function the more the myth will be encouraged and nurtured.

Racial difference, especially when it is as obvious as the difference between black and white, is a very natural focus for prejudice. But this natural tendency is blown up into a myth when it is able to support a desired social structure. This racial prejudice gets blown up into the huge racist myth in order to internalise the values which place and keep the whites at the tip of the power structure and the blacks at the bottom.

The history of the process of racism in South Africa would run something like this. When the land-hungry white invaders reached the Southern tip of Africa they encountered the blacks who regarded the land as their own. Very soon, therefore, conflicts arose over the land. But black technology was unable to match white technology in the art of warfare and so black resistance collapsed. The white victors now came to own the land and thus had access to the largest slice of the wealth of the country. This they liked so much that almost every politically important decision that has been taken since then has been to ensure the wealth and power privilege of the whites, and to reduce the threat of any competition for wealth and power from the blacks.

In this atmosphere of a power and money struggle the myth of racism grew. Whites had to believe that the blacks they were excluding were being rightly and righteously excluded. They even wanted blacks to come to believe this themselves. It is not surprising, therefore, that religion has been one of the major bastions and creators of the race myth of the inferiority and labour – or 'Ham' – quality of the blacks.

Since, however, the racist myth has grown up to lend 'internalising' and moral support to what is essentially a power struggle in which the *status quo* has been established by a violent struggle, it is clear that no radical social change will be brought about by attacking the myth without attacking the causes of the myth. It would be as useless to attempt to bring about social health by attacking the myth of racism as it would be to try to bring medical health to a leper by attacking the myths surrounding leprosy.

Similarly if racial prejudice exists as a myth to preserve a structure in which a few have a monopoly of power and wealth, then it is the concept of a few having a monopoly of power and wealth which must be attacked.

Power and Authoritarianism

Authoritarianism is the way in which power is structured in an on-going society without always having to resort to physical violence. It was in physical violence that power was wrested by the white from the blacks in South African history, While physical violence is by no means dead as a way of maintaining the *status quo* of the power struggle, the primary way has been to set up political structures in which authority to take certain decisions is vested in people because they hold that office. Thus we have everything from prime ministers down to police constables. They don't have to kill anybody to have power to decide and act for others. This is regarded as their right by virtue of their appointment to their office (and, of course, certain people are rigidly excluded from holding these offices).

This is authoritarianism. It is the social structure in which some people are regarded as having the right to exercise control over the lives of others by virtue of the position they hold within the social structure.

As such it is by no means limited to political structures. It is found in a home situation in which, as St Paul says, the husband is to be the 'head' of his wife (Eph. 5: 23). Here it is unimportant whether the woman is a better leader or wiser than her husband. All that is important is that there is an established pattern of authority and that the one who holds the 'office' of husband automatically has authority over the one who holds the 'office' of wife.

It is so also in ecclesiastical structures in which a hierarchy of authority structures is set up. At the 'top' is some form of Pope, Archbishop, President or Moderator. It is an 'office' to which a man is 'called' and appointed. In coming to his office this man also comes into certain powers, i.e. a position in which he is said rightly to exercise control over the lives of others.

There are many other examples of this in our society, but this should be enough to show the extent to which our society is criss-crossed with authoritarian structures which give some people the right to make decisions for others. In every instance the structure is supported by a myth. In the political power structure the myth of racism is crucial, as is also the myth of Communism – i.e. every person who questions this political structure is labelled a 'subversive communistic agitator'. In the family structure there are the host of myths about the character, strength and role of women – all of which serve to reinforce the idea that women should be the servants of men. In the Church there is the myth of 'divine election', which hardly masks the struggles for power that go on at election times, but which more or less successfully subdue the 'non-elect', i.e. the non-elected.

Authoritarianism and Inter-personal Relations

Racism as such is not the real poison in inter-personal relations. It is that for which racism exists, i.e. vast discrepancies in the distribution of power. Where societies have different offices enshrining and perpetuating power discrepancies, there will always be struggles between people aspiring to the offices. In their extreme form these struggles result in assassinations and *coups d'état*. In their less extreme forms they show themselves in jealousies, back-biting and tale bearing to 'higher powers'.

Within the Church too these power struggles are a sickening aspect of our life together. One can see this in its naked and un-sophisticated form in the brutal struggles for power in an organisation such as the African Independent Churches Association.* But it is far from absent in the major historic Churches. Here men, advanced to positions of authority over others, enter into interminable wrangles which cause bitter complaints among those over whom they have been set in authority.

All this is very understandable. However true it may be that people don't like taking responsibility and prefer to carry out the orders of others, it is also true that both adults and children do resist those in authority and like to feel that they are able to share in taking the decisions that affect them. The only time that most of us are happy with an authority figure is when we believe that there is a fair chance of being shown favouritism (hence political dictators always have their ring of favourite sons and ardent supporters, and children carry tales to their parents), or when the person in authority does what we would do if we were in power.

More important than the way we feel about those in authority is the fact that human relations depend on at least two human beings who are trying to work out the character of their re-lationship. But this requires that both should be authentically themselves, and the relationship depends on the sort of adjust-ments that each makes in order to continue to include the other in the relationship. The one may try to dominate the other – and the extent to which this happens will be the extent to which the relationship ceases to be an authentic two-way interplay.

* Formed in mid-1960s by some 300 of the 3,000 independent churches in South Africa, which have no links with the major world-wide denominations.

Consequently, while in an authoritarian structure there may be good relationships between the people involved when they operate outside the structure, there cannot be the same character of inter-personal give and take and involvement within the structure itself.

If, therefore, we are concerned about inter-personal relationships and thus also with personal freedom, then we cannot accept authoritarianism in any form. To reject racism and leave the authoritarianism basically unchanged may be to change the names of the people in 'office' but is unlikely to change the names or the lot of the people at the bottom of the power pile. And one of the main reasons for Black Theology is that black people are at the oppressed end of society. If all that is achieved is that black rulers replace white rulers but those at the 'bottom' experience very little change in their freedom and recognition, then there will still be a need for a Black Theology, or a eology of the oppressed.

thoritarianism and Black Society

n African society at present there is a strange mixture of rigid authoritarian patterns on one side and values and practices which are decidedly non-authoritarian on the other. Perhaps the most authoritarian facet is in the family, where the patriarch is the final and unquestioned authority. This is strongly supported by ancestor worship. The family head, as he gets older and older, gets nearer and nearer to death and emergence into the world of the ancestors. On the one hand this leads to a solicitous care for the aged, but on the other it imbues the older members with a power and authority which dare not be questioned without inviting dire consequences.

Yet at the same time it is true that decision-making in the society is not left entirely in the hands of headmen and chiefs. While women and children are excluded, the long and slow process of *indabas** is well known. There issues are discussed at length and decisions taken which filter slowly up through the society until they are gathered together and given legal force in the pronouncements of the chief. Here, at some point in the decision-making process, many are involved in making their contribution towards the final outcome. This does not

* Zulu word meaning discussion or council.

mean that people are free to break the consensus, but it simply means that the extent of participation in the political processes in African society is far greater than in Western society – greater even than in its political party so-called 'democracy', where all that happens is that a few people at the top make all the decisions. The ordinary man is expected simply to endorse those decisions once every five years or so.

Authoritarianism and Christianity

Christianity too is a strange complex of extreme authoritarianism and freedom. Much of our language concerning God shows him to be the authoritarian *par excellence*. We speak of him in terms most of which are variations of a supreme ruler: Master, Lord, King, Judge, Father, Supreme Being, Omnipotent, etc. At the same time man is pictured as one who should be in total submission, and thus our language sees him in variations of slave, servant, son, child, etc.

There can be no denying that in the mainstream of Western Christianity, God is regarded as having the inalienable right to rule over his creation. Thus the religious man is most of all characterised by the prized attribute of total obedience. The irreligious man is the one who manifests the crass evil of disobedience.

The implication here is that there is only one will in the cosmos that really matters, namely the Divine will. Every other will is to be brought into submission to this will. But this means that there ought to be no people who are authentically themselves.

Some may argue that this is good because people are basically and inherently selfish and acquisitive. It is true that there is something of this in us. But it is also true that few, if any, of us really desire to be alone without any need for the love, friendship and acceptance of others. We all live with two forces struggling within ourselves: the will to be ourselves, to 'do our own thing', and the will to include others in our living. And in most of us the 'selfishness' is balanced and checked by the desire to avoid a rejection by those whose lives we wish to share. The 'selfishness' thing is the urge to be our own unique selves, which sometimes gets out of hand. The 'community' thing is the urge to be surrounded by friends who accept and support us, which can also become sick in prejudiced exclusions of some from our 'fellowship'. The tragedy in man is not that he is basically selfish and acquisitive, but rather that our urge to express our own uniqueness is distorted and encouraged in our acquisitive society at the expense of our urge to fellowship.

In Christianity, however, we have an almost insanely pessimistic view of man. We pick on his will to uniqueness, call this evil, and falsely claim that it is the most basic of his drives. Then over against this we posit God as the only one whose will is good and then call on men to submit themselves totally to this will as the only hope of salvation. And in doing so we also posit God as the supreme authoritarian and thus provide a tremendous emotional support for our structures of authoritarianism. (For example, if God reveals his absolute demand to the Pope, why should the Pope not demand total allegiance to his declaration of the will of God?)

But while there is this strongly authoritarian streak in Christianity there is the other side, which is frequently in marked contradiction to the authoritarianism. There is the emphasis on the uniqueness of the individual. There is the call that no person should be in bondage to any other. There is the repeated assertion that in Christ we have been set free. Together with these goes our understanding of God. Our uniqueness is supported by God's love for each of us as individuals. We ought to be in bondage to no man, for none is our master save God. We are free in Christ, because in Christ all are brothers working together for the health of the whole body.

Now if we are interested in our uniqueness and our freedom as black people we must look again at the sources of our theology to speak a word of hope to our people.

Black Theology and Freedom

It is no longer new to point to the fact that in his incarnation Christ was identified with the oppressed and the poor of his time for their liberation. In Black Theology it is no longer new to point to the fact that it is the black people who are the oppressed and the poor of our day, and thus that it is meaningful to speak of the Christ as the one who is identified with the blacks for their liberation.

At the same time, if our analysis of racism is correct, we have to be very careful not to identify oppression with racism. Even non-racists can be oppressors. Protestants oppress Catholics and vice versa, Jews and Hindus oppress Muslims, Muslims oppress Jews, landowners oppress serfs, political demagogues oppress rural peasants. It is oppression that must concern us more than the fact that at present racism and oppression are 'heads' and 'tails' of the same coin. We have to ask how we can safeguard the value, integrity and uniqueness of the individual so that he can express freely who he really is. At the same time we have to ask ourselves how we can express our desire to live together with others in a fulfilling harmony that is neither crass individualism nor oppressing authoritarianism. And we have to build the answers we find into organisations that we create to build a new society. (It is no good setting up a strictly authoritarian structure and hoping that this will die a natural death once authoritarian *racism* has been destroyed. We are fools if we try.)

Thus our prime concern is to speak a word of hope to people without power. And this word of hope cannot contain any promise that one day they will have power over others – even those 'others' who oppress them now. It must be a hope that one day we will live together without masters or slaves.

If we take ourselves seriously when we say that Christ is he who is identified with the oppressed for their liberation, then we cannot go on to expect that Christ will still be identified with us when we have thrown off the shackles of oppression to become the new authoritarian controllers of the lives of others. Even within our own organisations, if there is anyone whose life we try to control, then we will have denied the possibility of Christ's identification with us. If Christ is the brother and friend of the oppressed, then he is such no matter what the nature of the oppression. Thus only as those who wish to live in a freedom for all in a community of loving give and take can we hope to speak of Christ as he who is with us.

In the light of this, Black Theology has a dual role, if it is to speak a new word of freedom to our power-mad situation. On the one hand it must reject all language about God which seems to make him out to be the authoritarian *par excellence.* This means a rejection of the various 'Master' images of God as well as the concepts of his controlling the lives of people and carrying the power to reward the obedient with heaven and to punish the disobedient with hell. None of these images and concepts allows us to be free and authentically ourselves in our relationship with God, and all carry within them the seeds of authoritarianism which will grow in those who claim access to the Divine Will and thus a rightful share in God's authority to reward and punish. In the place of these authoritarian images we should explore those images which speak of the suffering God who is identified with the oppressed in their suffering and who struggles in and with them to lift the burden of oppression. As such God is neither our servant, to be treated as we choose, nor our master, to treat us as he chooses, but our comrade and friend in the struggle for freedom.

Alongside this, however, Black Theology must point the way to the possibility of our living in freedom without authoritarian power structures in our society. As such it must be alive to authoritarianism wherever it exists and thus also to the myths which support it. It must reject the pessimistic view of human nature which says that it is so intrinsically evil that there is no hope, without losing sight of the fact that many people are evil and try to twist society to their own ends – sometimes even unwittingly. Thus, for example, it will reject Bantustan politics, not primarily because it is a creation of the racist white South African government, but because it is still an alien and authoritarian political structure. As such it will have to create new myths to keep others out of power, such as the myths of traditionalism and tribalism (e.g. only traditional Zulu chiefs can be Prime Ministers of the 'Zulu nation').

Some Practical Implications

Thus the task of Black Theology is to be an authentic prophetic voice of freedom. But we know also that our words cannot be of a distant future and our practice a compromise with the present evil situation. We have the task of translating our vision into present practice.

This means that we have to be on our guard in our own structures and organisations that we don't become authoritarians working in authoritarian structures, and creating our own new highly charged emotional myths. This means refusing to give a few selected people the right to make the important decisions which affect the life of the organisation and to refuse to draw up rigid policies, and then to use these to exclude people who are not fully convinced or who have slightly different ideas. It means also refusing to create a myth of 'blackness' by which people who agree are called 'black' and those who don't are called 'non-white'. We have had enough of these power and manipulative techniques. This does not mean that it is not right to use 'black' as a value concept, to refer not simply to pigmentation but also and more importantly to the positive values held of the drive to shake off the shackles of inferiority and oppression for the new way of dignity, self-esteem and liberation. It means that we must be on our guard against an in-group cliquishness in which the value term 'black' is reduced to a means of insult and discrediting. To use the term 'black' as a means of insult or praise is very often to cloud the issues and values at stake. And it is these alone which are important.

Psychologically it is true that people are more open to change if they feel themselves to be in a non-threatening atmosphere where there is the sense of acceptance. People retreat on to the defensive and harden their stance when they feel rejected or attacked. We should use no punitive measures, not even psychological punishment, for this too is an ugly facet in the development of authoritarian control. If we want a society which recognizes the values and uniqueness of each individual as well as the wellbeing of the community, we cannot afford to use methods which attempt to degrade or control people.

In place of authoritarianism our organisations should be as broadly based as possible. As many people as possible should share in making the decisions which they will be responsible for implementing, and the structures should be flexible enough to change with changing situations and decisions. And the structures should be seen as being there simply to make it possible to carry out a particular activity. Our methods should be those of persuasion and encouragement and our organisations marked by their openness to people.

This does not mean that our structures will be amorphous and directionless. It means that we recognise that at the roots of both good politics and sound religion are healthy interpersonal relations in which persuasion is more creative than power, and acceptance more enabling than insulting rejection, and listening as vital as telling.

These sorts of freeing organisations will not be inefficient. Africa has a value system which makes people more important than time and speed. The West has a value system which makes speed more crucial than people. Thus Africa knows that a religious service will begin when the people are ready. The West wants it to begin at 11.00 a.m. no matter what. Africa will sit through long discussions until the people know and are satisfied with the decisions taken. The West leaves decisions to a few at the top, and then sits out long time-consuming and personally destructive squabbles which flow in the wake of unpopular decisions. It is the wisdom of the person-value of Africa that should mark our organisations. We need the efficiency of good human relations, not speedy achievement. Thus we need organisations that are pliable to the needs, hopes, aspirations and initiatives of all those involved. We can do without rulers of people. In their place we need people of wisdom who can both speak and listen to people and embody their common mind.

This means that if we build a new black Church we will have no room for white-style bishops. If we have bishops at all they will be leaders of the people only to the extent that they have heard the people sufficiently clearly to be able to speak both for them (i.e. gather together their thinking) and to them (i.e. to respond meaningfully to their needs). We cannot have the authoritarians who try to tell us what we believe or what to believe and who have the power to reward or punish us. We need a Church which is authentically a Church of the people for their liberation.

15

BLACK THEOLOGY AS
LIBERATION THEOLOGY

by Ananias Mpunzi

(i) *The Two Faces of Freedom*

If we are to speak of Black Theology as liberation theology, we must try to make as clear as possible what is meant by 'freedom'. Freedom, it would seem, has two distinct though clearly interrelated aspects. There is what we might call its structural aspect and, equally important but often neglected, its attitudinal aspect.

I. THE STRUCTURAL ASPECT

By the 'structural' aspect we do not mean simply a description of actual or possible social structures, but actual or possible structures related to the human drives they are meant to serve. Thus we have to look at these basic drives to ask ourselves how society could be organised to give these drives room for expression. We will also have to look at unfreedom, i.e. how society is ordered to suppress our basic human needs. Thus in its structural aspect freedom is a vision. It is a dream. And it has to do with the way society is ordered and organised. This structure for freedom itself has two aspects.

First there is the aspect of the *individual*. This is the freedom of the individual to be himself and to express his own *uniqueness*. This is an important drive within all of us. None of us wishes to be, or to be seen as, nothing more than a cog in a machine or a digit in a system. We want to be ourselves and to be treated as uniquely ourselves. We want people to relate to ourselves not simply to the 'whole' of which we are a 'part'. But the concept of our individual uniqueness is also a relational concept, as should already be apparent. Our desire for uniqueness is not a desire for isolation. It is a desire for recognition as unique and for room in which to express our uniqueness. It thus includes others.

Thus the second aspect – the community – is introduced. If we have a strong desire to be and to express ourselves, we have an equally strong desire for community. None of us really wishes to be alone on his own desert island cut off from all human contact. We want and need people about us who love and accept us. The human need for acceptance and the fear of rejection are as strong as the human need to be unique and express ourselves in our uniqueness, and the fear of this being crushed in conformity.

Both these drives live together within us. Sometimes we long to express who we really are, and attempt to do so. When we do so, and the reaction of those whose acceptance we need is to reject us, then we tend to draw back from this isolation of our uniqueness into the safety of the community. At other times we feel the pressures of the community on us making us conform. Against this the individual in us rebels. Thus we all know within ourselves the polarity of the self and the community, and the pulls between the two in the two directions; the desire for solitude and the desire for company; the desire to be in our uniqueness and the desire to be in our community. In our experience these two drives usually balance each other. The one stands as a constant corrective of the other.

In society, however, either of these corrective drives can be played up almost to the exclusion of the other, the one comes to be regarded as more important than the other. In our South African society, and in the West generally, it is the drive for uniqueness which is distorted by being made an end in itself: it is the individual that really matters, and no one should be allowed to stand in the way of the individual being able to express himself. But, of course, as we all know, other individuals have to be taken into account since they are part of the society in which the first individual wishes to express himself. The natural tendency would be to take these others into account positively for the sake of acceptance by them. But where this is seen as a hindrance to self-expression they are taken into account negatively.

What becomes important now is not 'How can I both be myself and be accepted by others?' but 'How can I be myself without the interference, threat, or obstruction of others?' The answer to this in South Africa is well known. You try to get power (educational, economic, military, or police power) in order to prevent others getting in the way, and you try to rule out as many competitors as possible. Here racism is important. You legislate and take other steps to rule out as competitors a whole group of people, i.e. black people are discriminated against as a total group.

But individualism is not finished yet. It is necessary to inculcate a sense that it is right that one person should 'succeed' at the expense of others. Thus almost everything we do is made competitive – try to be at the top of the class, get elected 'footballer of the year' or president of the club, etc. And the usual bedmate of the competitive society is the acquisitive society. Thus 'success' becomes gauged in terms of 'victory' in the various competitions and also in the amounts of money and objects possessed. The 'successful' person is usually the person with 'position' and wealth.

In this sort of authoritarian, racist, capitalistic society the urge to uniqueness and self-expression has become crass individualism. This is a structural manifestation of human sickness.

As much as it is possible to put one individual above the community as a value, creating an authoritarian social structure, so it is also possible to attempt to swallow up the individual in the community or the group. Here the 'needs and interests of the whole community' are said to be more important than the needs and interests of any individual in the community. Conformity is the arch-virtue and non-conformity the cardinal and unforgivable sin. The individual exists to serve the community and its interests, and in this lies his value. His value is not in himself. If he fails to serve the interest of the community he is dispensible. In this *communal fascism* it is the decision of the group that really counts. The individual is not entitled to hold contrary views. If he tries he must be put down.

In South Africa one also finds this communal fascism. But it is markedly sectional. The white ruling group intensely desires unity against the black ruled group. While blacks who deviate from their position as the ruled are regarded as threats, the response of the white group is not nearly as hysterical as it is against white deviants. White deviants from white authoritarian conformity are seen as criminal threats against 'our way of life' as a closed community, cancerous growths within who will destroy the whole. This communal fascism which seeks rigidly to control the individual is not a prerogative of the white group only. It is an ever-present danger in the black group as well. Here the group seeks to exclude the deviant, the waverer – in fact anyone who seems to have a different point of view. In communal fascism the control by some of others is as important as it is in authoritarian individualism.

Neither authoritarian individualism nor communal fascism can ever be a structure for freedom. They are static structures for control. But freedom can never be a state; it is a process, for it involves the continual movement within ourselves to be in our uniqueness and to be in our community. If ever there is to be freedom it has to allow for this movement. It demands a tremendously high evaluation of human beings to allow them to *be* – both in their desire to be themselves and in their desire for acceptance into a living community.

This does not mean that there are not structures which can give greater life to this mobility and other structures that can destroy it. Our task is to look for the structures that can support freedom, though the structures themselves are not freedom. But they will be structures which are as flexible and adaptable as the human beings they are designed to serve. Within such structures no one will be given a position of power to control the lives of others, and there will be no rigid 'policy' decisions by which people will be judged. Instead, all those involved will share in taking the decisions that affect them. And while no one will be free to harm any other, those who wish to disagree or to opt out will be free to do so. What structures there are will be there simply as servants of people or as servants of any function or project. No structure should exist to perpetuate itself. It should exist only to achieve a certain purpose or to enable people as much as possible to explore the ever-increasing horizon of their freedom in their uniqueness and desire for community.

2. THE ATTITUDINAL ASPECT

While the structural aspect of freedom is not to be ignored as unimportant, it also must not be regarded as freedom itself. There is also a sense in which freedom is an attitude of mind which can exist in any situation or in any structure. Not only can it exist in any structure, it must exist in any structure if there is to be any change in the structures that enslave.

This attitudinal aspect is beautifully expressed by Solzhenitzyn in *The First Circle*. Nerzhin, indefinitely detained in prison, refuses to see the slops served to the prisoners as slops. They are a sacrament. Perhaps the deep significance of this is that slops are for pigs. Prisoners are served slops because they are seen as pigs and are being encouraged to see themselves as pigs. But the sacrament is for humans. To see the prison slops as a sacrament is thus a tremendous act of self-affirmation – despite the prison and despite the slops. It is the attitude of mind that says: 'Think what you will of me. I know myself to be a person. And I will not allow your attitude towards me or your actions against me to crush me. I will be what I am despite you – a person utterly intent on affirming my humanity.'

This is a crucial aspect for blacks in South Africa. We have been treated as less than human. We have been debarred from having a say in making the decisions that intimately affect our lives. Whites have come to see us as dogs (signs reading 'No dogs or Bantu' are not uncommon). Our blackness has been seen as the sign of our non-humanness. It stands for that which is dark and evil. Our past is seen as a past of barbarism. We are seen as little more than a troop of baboons with remarkably human-like features!

The tragedy is not simply that we have been served the slops for pigs. It is also that we ourselves have seen slops and thus ourselves as pigs. Thus our own self-affirmation has been bound and chained. When we cease to love ourselves we cease also to be able to love others. Love is a *give*-and-take relationship. What has a pig to give? Our self-denigration then becomes the reason for denigrating others, and we learn also to behave as pigs. Thus we destroy not only ourselves but others. First, like dogs in a pack, we turn on the others wounded among us, we turn against those who should be our brothers in suffering. Then we learn to hate and destroy those who have destroyed us.

Freedom, however, is that attitude which says: 'Our blackness is a sign of our humanness. It stands for our identity as people – a suffering people, whose suffering is so deep because it is human suffering.' Thus freedom also has this dimension of self-affirmation in whatever situation we find ourselves, the affirmation of ourselves in our blackness. We are *black people*. No one can take this from us.

But there is also a communal aspect in this. If we love and affirm ourselves it is not simply for ourselves but so that we can enter into the give-and-take of a healthy love with others. However, as little as we want to give our piggishness to others, so we do not wish to receive piggishness from others. We want to give ourselves as self-affirming people, and we want to receive into our being self-affirming people.

For our sakes, therefore, we have the task both of affirming the humanity of others and helping them to affirm it for themselves when it seems as if they have denied it. Thus freedom also entails enabling black people, all black people everywhere, to affirm what they are – *black people* – and enabling white people to affirm what they are – just *ordinary* people, even though they are white.

Having said what we mean by freedom in its structural and attitudinal aspects, we now need to turn to the theological dimension of these aspects.

(ii) *Black Theology and Freedom*

We have seen that by freedom is meant those structures which support and strengthen us in our uniqueness as individuals and in our desire for community – and that attitude of mind in which we affirm our humanity as individuals and the humanity of others who constitute the community.

Black Theology is a situational theology. It asks theological questions which are vital to particular people in a particular situation – that is, to us, the black people in South Africa – and the questions are the questions *we* are asking. Thus the 'theological dimension' is that which refers to *us* in our black situation.

First, then, does Black Theology support us in our drive to be ourselves in our uniqueness? Does it lend its support to our need to affirm ourselves as persons, as black persons? Thus is Black Theology a theology of liberation in this personal sense? To answer this we point to the doctrine of Creation. Whatever is meant by this doctrine it cannot be the *deus ex machina*; the God who set the mechanism ticking and now leaves it to run on its own. If that is what is meant, then God is not *my* Creator. He may be the Creator of my distant forbears, but not *my* Creator. No one could possibly be interested in a God at that distance, so mind-bogglingly removed from us in our here and now. The 'beginnings' referred to in the doctrine of Creation are surely no explanation of the present. They are not an explanation at all. It is the declaration of a relationship. It declares the immediacy of God's relationship with *me*. It affirms that God loves me as a unique individual as a father loves his children as unique individuals and that God has a unique will for me, not a general will for all into which I must fit, just as a father has specific hopes and dreams for each of his children as individuals, not a general desire for them all as a block.

Thus any affirmation of God must also be an affirmation of the uniqueness of every individual. If this affirmation of God is not simply to be pious and irrelevant talk, then it must also entail that I have the room in which to give visible expression to my uniqueness.

If this is what the doctrine of Creation entails, then it entails also the Divine affirmation of my uniqueness. And if a relationship of love is entailed between God and the unique individual, and if love is the give-and-take of a mutual honouring and self-honouring, then I have no right whatever to deny my unique personality in any way. It is an insult to God the Creator if ever anyone does deny it and a greater insult if we ever allow this behaviour by others to lead us on to think of ourselves as less than precious and unique individuals.

Thus, as Christians, we must affirm again and again that we are people. But people come in all sorts of different colours, shapes and sizes. My humanity includes my thinness, my fatness, my shortness, my tallness, my big nose, my small ears, my blackness or my whiteness. I am not a person *despite* my big nose. I am a person because the big nose, the small ears, the thin frame and the blackness are mine. Without the totality that is me I am not me! Therefore, in affirming my humanity I must affirm everything that is me. I must affirm my blackness. God must also affirm it, otherwise he could not know me or have any dealings with me, and my blackness would exclude me from him. It would exclude me from being a person. This does not mean that we must simply affirm everything about ourselves in a way that leaves no room for change. We must claim and affirm those things which we cannot change (such as our blackness) and we must acknowledge those things we can change (such as our attitudes to our blackness). Among the things we can change there will be those we must affirm as good without any apology. But there will be attitudes and values which we ourselves cannot accept as good. We need to acknowledge and understand these and to work at becoming new.

Thus Black Theology claims that God affirms my uniquneess, and so my blackness. It goes further and says: 'Black person, you are a unique person, and you must express your uniqueness or die, and you must affirm your humanity or become the thing, the object, that others have deluded you into believing yourself to be'. On the one hand you must tear down every man-made barrier that restricts your freedom to be yourself. and to live God's unique will for you in vibrantly fulfilling life. On the other hand, you must affirm yourself as a human being no matter what your situation or what others may say or do to you. You dare not believe the lies that others would make you believe by the nature of their non-human relationship with you. You dare only believe the truth that God would have you believe by the nature of his self-affirming relationship with you. You must love the sign of your humanity which others treat as the sign of your lack of humanity. You must love your own black body – your blackness!

Black Theology has no room for the traditional Christian pessimistic view of man, the view that we are all by nature overwhelmingly and sinfully selfish. We know only too well that our white Western acquisitive society tries to harness that good and beautiful and God-given thing, our self-awareness, self-esteem and longing to be ourselves in our uniqueness. It has tried to take this away from us and replace it by crass individual-

ism. Then the white, Western Church has come in alongside
this. It has said little and done less to change this pattern of
subversion of our self-pride. But it has ranted against those
who have fallen prey to its own devouring influence, and called
upon us to deny and denounce ourselves as people. 'We are
selfish, We are worms.' And we have believed this and then let
others trample over us. This pessimism about man is therefore
an ally in our own undermining of ourselves.

Black Theology will have no truck with this. It is true that
we are often deluded and duped, but our need to be ourselves
in our uniqueness and thus our blackness is not evidence of the
rampaging evil inherent in us. It is the stirring of God calling
us to be ourselves so that we might respond not as worms but
as people, both to God and to others. We must respond as
what we know ourselves to be: black people.

Black Theology is a powerful call to freedom for black people,
calling us to throw off the psychological shackles and structural
bonds that hold us in self-denying conformity and bondage to
others.

But there is also the relational dimension to freedom. Does
Black Theology call us also to freedom in this inter-personal
dimension both in its structural form and in its attitudinal
aspect? At the heart of the Christian doctrine of God is the
Trinity. Western theology has gone into metaphysical somer-
saults over this doctrine, but it is not a metaphysical doctrine.
It is deeply and passionately human. Would that we could
drop the ossified Greco-Roman credal confessions of the Trinity
and give new human life to the doctrine. The doctrine again
is not an hypothesis to explain anything. It is a vision of tomorrow, of people as they ought to be, not an explanation of
yesterday. Talk about the Trinity is not talk about a God 'out
there', but it is talk about the ultimate in human relationships.
It is thus a visionary call to the new.

On the one hand the doctrine affirms the uniqueness of the
'persons' of the Trinity. They are themselves and no others.
They are who they are. But at the same time – and this is vital –
they are one. God is not any one of the unique three alone.
God is the oneness of the community. And that community
demands an equality of the unique persons and their inter-
relationship. Their uniqueness grows out of and is expressed

in their unity. And that unity is God. It is in the image of this God that man is made, hence our humanity is not the sum and total of our uniqueness. It is not enough to say that we are persons in our uniqueness, however vital it is to say that. We are persons in the unity that holds people in the powerful give-and-take of love and acceptance.

Black Theology asserts that people, made in the image of the Trinity among whose three 'persons' there is no superiority, are not meant to set some up in authority over others to rule their lives. It says that man, with his longing for fellowship, will tear down every structure that sets about trying to rule over others; authoritarianism must be destroyed in every one of its manifestations, particularly its racialist manifestation.

The freedom of which Black Theology speaks thus demands an attitude of enormous respect for others, and that because of this attitude we will refuse to allow any man to humiliate himself because others choose to humiliate him. We must shout loud and clear and far and wide to anyone who will hear: 'You are persons made for love. Don't cut yourself off from that love by thinking and acting as if you were superior to anyone else, and especially by acting as if you were inferior to anyone else.' It demands also, however, that we bully no one; people are too precious. We dare not in this way destroy them and thus their uniqueness. But we will do everything else to make people stand up and be themselves in the community of self- and mutually-respecting people.

Thus Black Theology is a theology of liberation. Although it directs its voice to black people, it nonetheless hopes that white people also will hear and be saved. In its call to black people it says: 'You, black person, are unique. Your longing to express your uniqueness is the stirring call of God within you. So don't let anybody try to fence in your unique being. Throw off anything that would attempt to do so.' It also says 'You, black people, want and need a community of accepting love. This too is the call of God in your brother. Answer it, but do not bow down to your brother or you will make him not your brother but your king.' Thus it says: 'Share your living but do not sell yourselves. Love your brother and affirm him, but do not make him more than you.' And finally it says: 'Black person, you could not be you and not black. So affirm and love and glory in your blackness.'

When all of this is a reality within us we will be on the move again, and being on the move is the only state of freedom, for God is on the move. Freedom is not having arrived, it is not being God. It is rather struggling to arrive, it is struggling to understand and to respond to God – the God who is not yesterday's explanation but the vision of, and call to, tomorrow, and tomorrow, and tomorrow.

16

THE TRAINING OF
BLACK MINISTERS TODAY

by Sabelo Ntwasa

I will not attempt to examine in detail the present form of
theological education in our theological institutions in South
Africa, as it is common knowledge to all of us. The tendency
in almost all theological institutions is to try to produce pastors
and theologians, but whether this is done successfully is very
doubtful. These institutions produce men, after a period of
rigorous lectures on Doctrine, Ethics, Church History and the
New Testament, who find it very difficult, because of their
educational background, to weld all these theological subjects
into a meaningful Christian theology that can help them to
grow in their understanding of the Christian gospel in a given
situation, i.e. in their own black churches.

The aim of most of our theological colleges is to turn out
men with a sensitive theological perception and of good pastoral inclination. But do the various black centres for theological education succeed in doing this? My claim is that they don't.
The ordinary black student comes to the theological college
with all his prejudices from his own parish situation. At the
seminary he is often so shattered by the scientific approach to
the meaning of Christian theology that he is shaken in his faith.
The remark of one new student after his first encounter with
literary criticism of the Bible was: 'They are trying to destroy
our faith' While such a reaction is generally anticipated by
the staff, little is done to find out whether the students outgrow
it.

The packed syllabuses and frightening examination system
are still very much with us in our black seminaries. The heavy

lecture programme necessitated by the syllabus is no comfort
to the student, who mostly knows that his ordination may depend on his passing the examination. This state of affairs
leaves the student little time for reflection on the many new
theological truths he is encountering for the first time. Consequently the whole system of lectures, compounded by frequent
essay projects and the overriding fear of examinations, makes
the black seminary student a rather frightened little 'Pass
examination' kind of person who frequently fails to come to
terms with either Christian theology or the South African situation. Seldom are these two dynamically inter-related to provide
a basis for his ministry.

Let us look at the disciplinary code at most of our seminaries.
The black student finds himself having to 'behave' so that what
is lurking in his mind is the problem of how 'to keep the rules'
rather than 'what to do to make life at the college more meaningful to all concerned'. The mood of lack of total trust in the
staff is a constant problem. This does not mean that there is a
lack of acceptance of authority, but often that there is a lack
of complete confidence in those in authority because they are
white. A fellow black student seen frequenting the house of a
staff member, even if only because of personal affection for
each other, sometimes gives rise to remarks such as '*Wasigqiba*',
meaning 'he has finished us'; our reputations or position could
be threatened by this fraternising with one who is going to take
part in deciding our fate, i.e. ordination or no ordination. This
leads to a belief among those very few who don't feel like this
that the aim of most black theological students is to get a collar
at all costs.

In this situation, how does one think undisturbedly about
the significance of one's theological education in relation to the
parish situation one is to fill on leaving college? It is not surprising that a frightened little theological student becomes the
authoritarian in the parish. When his pattern of behaviour in
the seminary is that of subservience to (white) authority, it is
natural that when he leaves the seminary he reproduces the
same pattern in the parish, himself replacing the white authority figure, to become the one who must be listened to and
obeyed. Further, because he has failed to gain clear insight
and direction for his ministry at college, he cannot afford to

have his decisions questioned or discussed in the parish; he is too insecure for this. He cannot even afford to share decision-making with others, for this might reveal his shaky foundations. Consequently he must act as one who has the monopoly of truth and insist that he be treated as such. His only alternative is to allow himself to be crushed in the parish situation.

A review of our black seminaries is not only right, but long overdue. Such a review would need to look seriously at the general life-style prevailing there and the theological content of the training. It should, quite consciously, take into account black education and the socio-political situation of the country generally and black parishes in particular.

The black student comes to the seminary having been shoved through a system of education which makes a virtue of swotting and the uncreative regurgitation of his teachers' notes. In the system original thinking and the use of critical faculties are impossible. Familiarity with this method of indoctrination often makes the student feel that this is what education is about.

If our seminary training is able to give students the basic equipment to go on to higher degrees, all to the good. But if this is done while at the same time the black student is made incapable of reaching a theological (and secular) understanding of his socio-political situation, on the basis of which he can plan a significant ministry to his people in the black parishes, then it is at best irrelevant and at the worst positively harmful.

So the black student comes into a new educational world in the seminary, where it is at least claimed that the student is required to think for himself. This in itself creates a sense of insecurity, which is heightened by the fact that the majority of the seminary staff are white. In South Africa whites not only regard themselves as superior and rightfully in authority, but many blacks reinforce that view. Intellectually blacks may reject the plea of an unquestionable right of whites to authority, but emotionally this attitude is extremely difficult to discard. Hence it is difficult for students to put into effect the claim that they are required to think for themselves.

The problems do not end here with the white staff/black student seminary situation. The white staff are frequently highly competent academically, at least when judged by the standards and requirements of Western universities. None of them, however, has any existential knowledge of what it is to be a black man in white racist South Africa, and so it is impossible for them to think theologically from the basis of this human experience common, in varying degrees, to all South African blacks. This is bad enough, but it is still not all. Few, if any, of them have any first-hand experience of either black communities or black parishes in their living or work situation. Those who have not come to the seminaries from overseas have experienced South Africa from the situation of the white suburbs. Hence it is to be expected that the pastoral training in the seminaries is inadequate. In any event students have little confidence that the white staff are able to think creatively about the application of Christian theology in black parishes and thus to prepare black students for their role as pastors and community leaders. Consequently it is not surprising to find very few changes in the traditional patterns of black parish ministries.

At the moment it would not be unfair to say that the most positive contribution of our seminaries is to enable students to reach a sufficient level of competence to study abroad (i.e. in white Western academic institutions). These students can study the Bible in the original languages and learn something about Church history, the historical debates on doctrine, and doctrine itself. But as creative agents for change in the South African Church embedded in the South African sociopolitical situation they will have largely failed.

What is the way ahead? This is an easy question to ask but, of course, very difficult to answer. Yet an answer must be attempted and, I believe, it will be in the interests of all blacks concerned with Christianity to look seriously at black theological training – that is, if the Gospel of Christ is to have any significance for or effect on our black community.

I shall now be bold enough to make a few suggestions.

First there is the question of the selection of men for theological training. If it is our wish to have men in our midst who are serious about black liberation, then we (the Church) must be sure that in our selection of ordinands we select the right people, namely those whose motives are for the liberation of black people and who see this as an essential aspect of the meaning of salvation. At present the Church has enough Uncle

Toms amongst its clergy: we should work to decrease rather than increase their number. If the Church is to become the Church with a prophetic voice it needs prophets. These cannot be mass-produced but you can at least try to ensure that those being trained are not there because they see the ministry as the gateway to a middle-class life. Our life as ministers of Christ ought to be one of identification with the wretched of the earth (i.e. in South Africa with its impoverished black community).

Consequently, the selection of a black ordinand should be based on some evidence that he sees himself as part of the black community, with whom he shares a longing for liberation. Selection should also be based on some evidence that he sees his training as leading him to a fuller understanding of liberation in terms of which he is able to plan his ministry of service.

Secondly, and flowing out of this, we have the duty to provide the sort of training for black ordinands which will meet the criteria for selection of ordinands. If the Christian Gospel is about liberation from sin, then it is not simply about liberation from individual, personal, private sins (like swearing or fornication) but also about liberation from the social sins which dehumanise and debilitate people – especially black people in South Africa. The vast majority of our black people suffer shockingly under the impact not simply of racism but of poverty, hunger, ignorance and disease. The problems of most of our people are immediate 'bread and land issues'.

At present, while our ex-seminarian may be able to read his New Testament in Greek and to forward moral arguments for or against extra-marital sex, he is totally unequipped to help his people even breathe under the yoke of poverty. Would there not be some value in focusing both theologically and practically on the care of natural resources (such as land, crops, water, animals and human bodies) so that they can be used by people to carve out for themselves a more fully human life?

My third point, which is an aspect of the second one, is the question of human dignity and self-esteem. Almost everywhere blackness has gathered around itself a host of negative connotations: it is evil, ugly, sinful, dark, not-to-be-trusted, ignorant, and so on. In South Africa the ruling white people have carried all these negative connotations over on to the black people. At the worst the Church has been party to this, and at the best it has tried to ignore pigmentation. But even the latter attitude has not enabled people to accept their blackness, and the historico-cultural background that goes with it, positively and naturally. Black men are black men; they don't have to prove their humanity despite their blackness.

This means that black seminaries ought to be able to look at the doctrine of men not simply in idealistic and utopian terms. This element should not be ignored, but neither should the situational facts. In this situation huge social and emotional consequences flow from being born black, most of which are negative, debilitating and dehumanising. Black students ought to be encouraged and enabled to focus at least theologically on their blackness, which entails looking back and re-assessing black history, black culture, black traditions and black beliefs (or, more accurately, African beliefs) looking at the present and assessing the theological and secular realities of the black experience, and looking to the future and our Christian goals. In the light of all of this our seminary students might be enabled to plan a relevant and significant ministry.

Finally, if any of this is ever to happen we will need to look seriously and critically at what we regard as adequate criteria for the selection of seminary staff. At present our white-dominated churches tell us that it is an accidental circumstance that most of the seminary staff are white. This is the way it has to be when the criteria of competence set up by these white-dominated institutions are taken from Western models. But are these the criteria demanded by our black situation? Surely criteria such as an intimate knowledge of the black history, culture, community, parish, experience and aspirations are at least equally important. If such criteria were set up and applied, it might become an accidental circumstance that most of the seminary staff would be black. I am not arguing for racial criteria of selection, but simply for the application of criteria which will more adequately meet our situational needs.

These are but exploratory probings by a mere theological student who happens to be black. They are addressed primarily at other black theological students in the hope that they will spark off debate, criticism and discussion of the role of black seminarians who are on the way to becoming black clergymen.

17

THEOLOGICAL GROUNDS FOR AN ETHIC OF HOPE

by Manas Buthelezi

Hope is one of the basic spiritual ingredients that serve to enhance the quality of human life. Life without a dimension of hope is but a caricature of the divine gift of creation about which the Bible dramatically reports: 'Then the Lord God formed man of dust from the ground and breathed into his nostrils the breath of life; and man became a living being' (Gen. 2: 7). Where man lives without hope there is lacking a clear appreciation of the value and purpose of life itself. Life lacks any dimension of quality.

A suicide is one who has so completely lost the sense of value and purpose in his continued existence that he does not hesitate to see as his immediate duty the termination of his own life. A habitual criminal or saboteur of social order is one who, among other things, has subconsciously so lost the appreciation of what society at large regards as culturally and morally good and worthy of preservation that he sees nothing wrong in undermining it.

A considerable amount of the goodness and order in God's world has been wrecked by men without hope. Indeed sin itself is a pool in which the hopeless wallow. To speak of a hopeless society is a contradiction in terms. Hopelessness and social order are mutually exclusive concepts. Hopelessness – meaning the loss of a wholesome vision of what is and is to be – is a sure gateway to anxiety and panic.

The Christian Gospel is designed to fill man with hope in order that he may realise that life is worth living and that he has a role to play in improving the quality of the life of his fellow-men – in particular, by filling them with the same hope which has sustained him.

We shall here address ourselves to the socio-ethical content of hope by characterising its theological basis. We will thereby highlight the theological ingredients of a socio-ethical outlook which breeds the hope which is so necessary to a dynamic social order. For the purpose of our discussion we have isolated two interrelated theological concepts, first Faith in God and secondly Faith in God's world. We will merely outline a theological approach; details of practical application and implementation will not be our immediate concern. In the first section we shall show how faith in God through Christ has an ethical dimension of hope that has a bearing on daily life. The concept of the body of Christ will be used in order to demonstrate that a dynamic Christian discipleship derives from a feeling of security and a sense of belonging to a corporal solidarity anchored in Christ. In the final section our aim will be to show how faith understood as acceptance of God's grace has a socio-ethical perspective which we have dubbed 'faith in God's world'.

(i) *Faith in God*

Hope is inseparable from the other two members in the Pauline trinity of virtues, namely faith and love (1 Cor. 13: 13). It is one facet of the tripartite 'Christian heart'. The dynamics of the Christian life are such that it is almost impossible to determine at all precisely where hope ends and where faith and love begin. Yet we shall abstract hope and discuss it against its divine basis and object. Its inner relationship with faith and love will, however, remain apparent throughout.

The reality of sin that engulfs man in his social setting accounts for his conscious or subconscious experience of anxiety and estrangement. He is torn both within himself and apart from God and his fellow-men in the context of God's creation. This alienation creates in him the feeling of insecurity, because his life is dislocated from its anchor or, to use a phrase of Tillich, its ground of being. The human experience of the threat and dread of death is the epitome of his existential feeling of insecurity and dislocation. We shall elaborate on this later. After describing the conflicting spiritual forces that vie in man, Paul exclaims: 'Wretched man that I am! Who will deliver me from this body of death? Thanks be to God through Jesus Christ our Lord.' Rom. 7: 24–25).

Later Augustine also underlined this truth in his classic statement that man's heart is restless until it finds rest in God who is the Creator of man. Man's restlessness takes many directions including the creation of human anchors of security. If man delays in finding the true God on whom to rest his hope, he does not hesitate to create gods after his own image. 'When the people saw that Moses delayed to come down from the mountain, the people gathered themselves together to Aaron, and said to him, Up, make us gods, who shall go before us; as for this Moses, the man who brought us up out of the land of Egypt, we do not know what has become of him.' (Ex. 32: 1)

The people of Jahweh made the Golden Calf as a substitute for the ethos of the Ten Commandments anchored on Jahweh. It is important for us to remember that the giving of the Ten Commandments was tied to a future promise: 'If you will obey my voice and keep my covenant, you *shall be my own possession* among all peoples; fu₁ all the earth is mine, and you *shall be to me a kingdom of priests and a holy nation*'. (Ex. 19: 5–6)

The original non-theological Hebrew meaning of covenant was an arrangement between two unequal partners of which the more powerful bound himself to a certain attitude towards the less powerful provided certain conditions were fulfilled by the latter. Even in theological usage, this element of the concept is retained as the above reference in Exodus shows. Jahweh is the initiator and sole benefactor in the covenant relationship. Israel's role is only to enjoy the benefit of the steadfastness of Jahweh's promise provided it remains faithful to Jahweh in hopeful anticipation of the fulfilment of that promise. The medium of 'promise' and 'fulfilment' is faithful participation in a community life whose ethos emanates from Jahweh's sovereign will. It is an ethos of hope since it is animated by Jahweh's promise whose fulfilment is already realised in hope.

Even though the New Testament uses different theological frames of reference, the basic pattern of relationship between God and man is retained. The radically new factor is Jesus Christ who *is* the ethos of the new community. According to John, Jesus says: 'I am the way, and the truth, and the life.'

(14: 6) Because Christ is the ethos of the new community, Paul can speak of the Church as the body of Christ. (Col. 1 : 18) Behind this figure is the Hebraic notion of 'corporate personality' in which a member of a family unit or tribe stands and acts for the entire social unit of which he is a member. The individual and his family, for instance, form an organism which is so closely knit that no single part of it can be separated and regarded as independent.

It is significant that when Paul introduces the section on Christian ethical responsibility in Romans he uses the analogy of the body in which each member plays a unique and necessary role for the benefit of all (Rom. 12). The ethical role of the members in the body of Christ should be seen against what Paul has said earlier in the sixth chapter concerning 'dying and rising with Christ' in baptism. Here the ethical implication is that Christian life is life after Christ. What happened to Christ, the new head of the human body, should happen to all its members, seeing that this has indeed already taken place in a sacramental fashion. Life in Christ follows the path that leads to victory after winding through the tunnel of suffering. Against the background of his own experience, Paul sums up this paradox in the Christian ethic thus: 'We are treated as impostors, and yet are true; as unknown, and yet well known; as dying, and behold we live; as punished, and yet not killed; as sorrowful, yet always rejoicing; as poor, yet making many rich; as having nothing, and yet possessing everything.' (2 Cor. 2: 8–10)

The Christian ethic is essentially an ethic of hope. Its context of realisation is the 'now' and the 'not yet'. The struggle against oppression coexists with the consciousness of victory as a realised eschatological event. That is why the delay in the manifestation of fruits does not detract from the intensity of a genuinely Christian ethical endeavour. The boundary between faith and hope melts away: while faith affirms the reality of the present, hope affirms the future reality as already present.

The knowledge that God in Christ, who has called us to follow him under all circumstances, is also Lord over all situations breeds a sustaining hope. Seen from the angle of the sovereignty of God and occasional Christian experience, life is a unique entity that defies any artificial division into parts. We may forget that we have a responsibility to inspire hope among not only those who are struggling in the Church, but those too who toil in life situations not ordinarily regarded as Christian.

Time and time again the Christian tries – often with apparent success – to run away from the hard and harsh realities of daily life and to withdraw into his spiritual ecclesiastical ghetto. If he is honest with himself, he sooner or later discovers the stark ineluctability of common daily life. But the discovery of solidarity in alienation and of the wholeness of life lead him to see that in life there are common strands that stretch across the boundaries between believer and non-believer. The Christian discovers that, as man, he still drinks the water that non-Christians drink, and tills the soil in which they too grow their crops. He finds himself toiling alongside his 'unbelieving' kinsmen fighting the natural forces of bad weather and barren soil, and disease and hunger. Indeed, he shares with them almost all the stigmata of alienation. He may have realised that life is a ball of fire which keeps on rolling towards him. He tries to run away from it but discovers that he cannot escape it because he is in it. In the arena of daily life he needs a hope that sustains him alongside his unbelieving brother, a 'courage to be'.

We do not precede life, but we find that life is already waiting for us. This is true both in its biological and societal manifestations. Life precedes us because God, who is the ground of life and before whom we live and exist, is there before us, waiting with his gifts. The theological consciousness of the givenness of the social, economic and political structures of life is not one of a fatalistic resignation, but of awareness of an inevitable responsibility in those structures. This is so because to have life does not mean just to be alive, but also to contribute critically and creatively to one's neighbour's well-being. It is this critical and creative shaping of the efficiency of the social structures which can instil hope among those who need it most, be they Christian or non-Christian.

(ii) *Faith in God's World*

Just as the fact of sin explains man's alienation from God, so does it also account for the alienation of man from man. It follows that salvation does not only consist in reconciling man with God but also includes reconciling man with man. This latter dimension has been lost from our concept of salvation partly as a result of the influence of the theology of Pietism. It is unnecessary to point out that this has resulted in an unfortunate narrowing of the hope of salvation so well enunciated in the Bible, e.g. the hope for Messianic peace and cosmic reconciliation in passages like Isaiah 11:6ff as well as New Testament references to love and peace among men as concomitant with salvation in Jesus Christ (Luke 2:14, John 13:34).

It takes faith in what God has done in Christ to reconcile man with God. Similarly it takes faith in what *man has become in Christ* to reconcile man with man. In forgiveness God accepts the sinner into his divine fellowship for the sake of Christ. In faith the sinner accepts God's forgiveness or acceptance as a reality that pertains to his personal existence.

Man's acceptance of God's acceptance must include the acceptance of all things which God accepts. What does God accept? He accepts the objects he has created as being worthy of mediating his grace to man. This is true whether we think of sacramental grace or the means he uses to preserve and sustain life in general. For instance, through the mechanical acts of eating and the ensuing physiological processes of digestion and assimilation, the presence and continuity of empirical life is mediated. As we have said earlier, in forgiveness God accepts fallen man into a living fellowship with him. He so accepts man that he even uses him to carry out his will in creation. The most obvious use of man by God is procreation wherein God accepts man, as it were, as co-creator.

Therefore in accepting what God has accepted, man accepts other men into his fellowship. It is against this background that we speak of faith in the world as a basis for an ethic of hope. The elements of this basis are as follows. First, man accepts created reality as the sphere over which God has placed him to have dominion; man exercises this dominion in the creative works of art and technology. (Gen. 1:28ff) Secondly, man accepts his neighbour as the one towards whose welfare all his efforts in this life are directed. Man in faith is man for others. His new freedom in Christ does not manifest itself in glory and power over others, but in self-giving and love for others.

Faith is at stake here, in that it is impossible to love someone whom you cannot trust. When we trust God in faith, we experience freedom and serenity in our being, akin to the consciousness of self-identification with the object of our love in self-surrender and service. To serve one's neighbour means to identify oneself with him and take his place in doing what he cannot do for himself.

In serving your neighbour, you vicariously become him in the sense in which Christ became ourselves on the Cross. It is thus impossible to love someone whom you despise and distrust. Love informed by faith acknowledges that the object of your love, by virtue of its being, is worthy of your identification of your being with it. This does not rule out the possibility of performing acts of love towards a person in whom you do not have faith when it comes to the question of recognising the worth of his being *vis-à-vis* your own being. Here lies the danger of speaking glibly about 'doing service to God'. In certain instances man is used as a means to an end in deeds of 'love' rendered as 'service to God'. No such act can be morally valid if it is performed towards a person in whose very manhood you do not have faith.

Morality finds meaning in recognising the worth and striving to achieve the wellbeing of a neighbour, rather than in a fastidious God taking pleasure at seeing man obey the laws he has capriciously made. Morality does not exist outside the context of life as it is lived, but it is the mainstay of societal life wherever it is found.

The morality of an act is determined by the extent to which its performance promotes the neighbour's wellbeing. Such promotion of wellbeing is consistent with the will of God, because God is above all things *for* the wellbeing of man – in Christ he has made an offer of forgiveness and acceptance of man. There is no generic difference between preaching to man the saving Gospel of Christ and serving man in response to those other necessities of life which promote his wellbeing within the given life structures and contribute towards his realisation of the wholeness of life.

Let me illustrate what I mean by the realisation of the wholeness of life and the promotion of the wellbeing of man. From time to time historical Christianity has ingeniously discerned some spiritual blessing in the occurrence among believers of such social ills as poverty and disease. This insight has ranged from the radical monastic glorification of poverty as an ethical ideal to the mild Protestant view of poverty as a blessed occasion through which God conveniently brings his spiritual gifts to the victim and stimulates the hearts of his saints to the making of material gifts of charity. Institutionalised charity is based on the tacit recognition of the poor as *bona fide* members of an established social class. The social function of charitable giving comes to consist in making the social horror of poverty less horrible, and a tenable medium of existence along with other social strata. Indeed, knowing no better life, the poor may live a life of happiness in their poverty, especially if they get occasional doses of charity.

Far from showing the poor that poverty is a form of alienation from the wholeness of life, the Church, in its pastoral counselling, has encouraged them to regard the possession of the material goods of life as, at best, a matter of indifference and, at worst, prejudicial to Christian growth. The poor were indirectly encouraged to be satisfied with their state of poverty. The assumption, of course, was that Christian charity would make up what they lacked of the material necessities of life.

The words of one of Paul Gerhardt's popular hymns, which is sung in my church, run thus in paraphrase: 'Be silent and do not grumble, you, poor one, when you see others around you who have more material possessions than you. You should know that you are richer and better off than they since you believe in God. After all, the things of this world are passing; we are pilgrims here and our real and ultimate home is in heaven.'

Of course, one can argue that spiritual goods are qualitatively more important than material ones in the nourishment of the Christian life and that 'man cannot live by bread alone'. But does it follow that a man can live a balanced life with the Word of God alone just as long as he gets the barest minimum of the necessities of life? We have to remember that the material goods of life are as much a gift of God as the Word; they are part and parcel of our creaturely existence in this world, and it is not only the rich who need them. Together with the Word, they constitute means for the realisation of the wholeness of life. Therefore, the Word of God cannot legitimately be pitted against them, even in the interest of giving spiritual counsel to the poor. The question whether the Word of God is more important for man than material things has only relative validity, since different necessities of life are involved.

The Gospel of hope for the condemned sinner cannot be fully grasped apart from the ethic of hope for a socially displaced victim. Our illustration of poverty is a case in point. Wherein lies the hope of a poor man assuming that he like others believes in Christ? In charity? We have referred to a situation where poverty provides an occasion for the display of charity. Shall the poor continue in poverty so that charity may abound at the sight of poverty's victims? God forbid. How can so highly priced a love feed on human victims? To shed light on the perspective of hope which these questions suggest, let us give a brief theological analysis of poverty.

Man's creaturely relationship to God is a given factor of his existence. For man, to exist means the same thing as to be a creature of God. Thus creatureliness, the result of the putting man in the world of created things, is descriptive of man's dependence on God. To live means to be at a point in God's creation where one receives and shares with others the life-sustaining gifts of creation, which are a complementary part of human existence. To be cut off from these gifts is an aspect of alienation from the wholeness of life. This, as a social phenomenon, is known as poverty – a situation of hopelessness.

It is within the given social structure of human existence that we receive God's gifts of life. We cannot by-pass what is around us and what has already been given in life in order to be at a point where God can bestow his gifts on us. Life in its social, economic and political setting is our only meeting-place with God. It is at this point that God gives us food, children, health, protection, the means of grace, and so on. Because of this the world around us becomes alive with God. Poverty is a state of displacement from this meeting-place with God, the place where he comes to distribute gifts to his children. The passport to this meeting-place is the opportunity for education and employment, and a character of diligence.

Hope for a poor man does not consist only in the removal of the symptoms of displacement – the effect of charitable giving – but in providing the poor with the passport to the meeting-place with God. Throughout the history of the Christian Church the act of the Good Samaritan has been recognised as the supreme exemplar and definition of a Christian act of love towards one's neighbour. This has an additional reason in that the parable dramatises the nature of sacrifice which transcends ethnic differences and taboos. A characteristic quality of the act of the Good Samaritan is the selfless response to a *situation of crisis*. The victim of the situation is transformed into a neighbour.

One may pertinently ask here whether in order to be *an ethical situation,* a situation of crisis necessarily has to be one which has run rampant to such an extent that it has engulfed human victims? Does the act of love necessarily consist only in rescuing casualties of a *situation of crisis?* Is it not also an act of love to *forestall* a situation of crisis for the sake of a neighbour who is its *potential* victim?

Our ultimate ethical responsibility is not only to serve man by removing the symptoms of alienation from the wholeness of life, but to equip him with the tools whereby he will be able to stand on his own feet. In this manner we shall be instilling in him courage to be himself so that he may take his place at a point in life where God continuously gives gifts to his children. He will begin to have faith in himself as a man after we have had faith in him as our fellow-man, that is, after we have 'accepted' him as a fellow-participant in the wholeness of life. We shall then all have something to live for – a hope that life is worth living. This is no Utopian dream since it is part and parcel of the ethic of Jesus who ministered to the whole man and said to the paralytic (Matt. 9: 2): 'Take heart, my son, your sins are forgiven.'